THE A–Z OF PRIMARY ENGLISH

MICHELLE NICHOLSON
SERIES EDITOR: ROY BLATCHFORD

Together we unlock every learner's unique potential

At Hachette Learning (formerly Hodder Education), there's one thing we're certain about. No two students learn the same way. That's why our approach to teaching begins by recognising the needs of individuals first.

Our mission is to allow every learner to fulfil their unique potential by empowering those who teach them. From our expert teaching and learning resources to our digital educational tools that make learning easier and more accessible for all, we provide solutions designed to maximise the impact of learning for every teacher, parent and student.

Aligned to our parent company, Hachette Livre, founded in 1826, we pride ourselves on being a learning solutions provider with a global footprint.

www.hachettelearning.com

Although every effort has been made to ensure that website addresses are correct at time of going to press, Hachette Learning cannot be held responsible for the content of any website mentioned in this book. It is sometimes possible to find a relocated web page by typing in the address of the home page for a website in the URL window of your browser.

Hachette UK's policy is to use papers that are natural, renewable and recyclable products and made from wood grown in well-managed forests and other controlled sources. The logging and manufacturing processes are expected to conform to the environmental regulations of the country of origin.

To order, please visit www.HachetteLearning.com or contact Customer Service at education@hachette.co.uk / +44 (0)1235 827827.

ISBN: 978 1 0360 0507 8

© Michelle Nicholson 2025

First published in 2025 by
Hachette Learning,
An Hachette UK Company
Carmelite House
50 Victoria Embankment
London EC4Y 0DZ
www.HachetteLearning.com

The authorised representative in the EEA is Hachette Ireland, 8 Castlecourt Centre, Dublin 15, D15 XTP3, Ireland (email: info@hbgi.ie)

Impression number   10 9 8 7 6 5 4 3 2 1
Year   2029 2028 2027 2026 2025

All rights reserved. Apart from any use permitted under UK copyright law, no part of this publication may be reproduced or transmitted in any form or by any means, electronic or mechanical, including photocopying and recording, or held within any information storage and retrieval system, without permission in writing from the publisher or under licence from the Copyright Licensing Agency Limited. Further details of such licences (for reprographic reproduction) may be obtained from the Copyright Licensing Agency Limited, www.cla.co.uk

Illustrations by DC Graphic Design Limited, Hextable, Kent.
Typeset in the UK.
Printed in the UK.

A catalogue record for this title is available from the British Library.

To my dear husband, who has supported me in my chosen profession for 40 years. You are my rock.

CONTENTS

About the author vi
Foreword by Roy Blatchford vii
Introduction x

Section One
Agency 3
Bibliophage 9
Craft 15
Decoding 23
Editing 31
Fluency 39
Grammar 47
Handwriting 55
Independence 61
Journey 69
Knowing 77
Library 85
Modelling 93
Networks 101
Oracy 109
Punctuate 117
Question 125
Reading 133

Sleuthing 141

Tenacity 149

Underserved 157

Verse 165

Wordsmiths 173

Xylophone 181

Yacht 187

Zeal 195

Section Two

1. Bibliophage 205
2. Editing 207
3. Fluency prompts 213
4. Handwriting 215
5. Models 219
6. Oracy 221
7. Spelling: accuracy with common exception words ... 223
8. Verse 225
9. Vocabulary and morphology 227

References 229

ABOUT THE AUTHOR

Michelle has amassed over 30 years of primary teaching experience since reading English literature and education at Homerton College, Cambridge. She has worked across a mixture of settings: as a class teacher, leading teacher, senior leader and education consultant. Michelle currently works as the Lead Primary English Adviser for HFL Education, supporting schools around the country to improve learning outcomes for children, and is a fellow of the Chartered College of Teaching.

Michelle is dedicated to ensuring all children can enjoy success in reading and writing, no matter what their circumstance. To this end, her master's degree research examined the psychology of learners and strategies to close the learning gap for our most vulnerable children. She supported schools as part of the National Strategies campaign Every Child a Writer, as well as working for the Herts Traveller Education Project and the national charity Achievement for All.

FOREWORD

In *Four Quartets*, T.S. Eliot testifies that success in language is a partial business, 'a new beginning, a raid on the inarticulate', at best a muddled string of attempts to define and redefine the nature of one's being, to rationalise its presence in society.

George Steiner, one of the outstanding linguists of the 20th century, wrote exhaustively on the global challenges of language, of which those of English are but a significant enclave. Why are there 4000 or more languages, he asks? Why, by a factor of a thousand, are there more languages than human blood types?

Every people has some variant on the Tower of Babel in its mythology. There exists a proliferation of neighbouring tongues that has been one of the most intractable barriers to human collaboration and economic progress. Arguably, in a digital and mobile phone age, we speak more to say less; we hear more and listen less.

This is the global context within which the English language is taught and learned in our schools.

Of all language activities, writing is the most artificial and the one with which most of us struggle from time to time. No wonder then that children should find writing problematic and that they should be surrounded with assumptions and popular shibboleths about how it can be taught and improved.

Writing imposes demands on the performer that do not characterise in the same way either our other active use of language (talking) or our receptive ones (reading and listening). And just as we cannot wholly know or evidence what we are going to say on paper until we have written it, so it is with speech; our recognitions and perceptions are less articulate, less explicit before they are shared.

Language in action comprises vocabulary, phonology, grammar, tone and emphasis. We can alter our meaning by being polite, aggressive or tentative and by modifying tonal quality, timing, stress and juncture.

Speech is a process of censoring, changing in mid-stream, restarting, irrelevant interrupting, hesitating and delaying monosyllabic utterances.

The business of speech and language is complicated and we probably take it for granted. 'It just comes naturally,' the saying goes. But for millions of children in our schools, speech and language do not flow naturally at all. From its own extensive research, the national charity Speech and Language UK estimates that approaching 2 million children and young people have obstacles to fluency. As these pupils progress through their school years, these obstacles damage self-esteem and certainly hinder academic progress.

My own researches in chairing the Association of School and College Leaders' commission The Forgotten Third identified fractured literacy and oracy at the heart of many students' academic and examination difficulties.

It is a sad reflection on the English schooling system that if the national inspectorate plays a certain tune, then all schools dance to that tune. Ofsted's focus on reading is testimony to that – and in fact that is proving to be no bad thing.

But before reading and writing, there are speech and language, and as a school system we need to get much better at developing all pupils' skills in this arena. This begins with families at home and is then a vibrant and vital continuum from ages 3–18.

An ambitious raid on the inarticulate needs to underpin every primary, special and secondary classroom, every day. Our children and young people deserve nothing less if they are to enter society as confident, conversational human beings.

****

In common with all titles in this A–Z series, Section One is orchestrated around the 26 letters of the English alphabet. Section Two offers a wealth of additional teaching and learning materials for the primary practitioner. The author has a command of subject – whether oracy, reading, writing, poetry, prose, fiction, non-fiction – that shines through on every page.

Michelle Nicholson takes the reader on an authoritative journey from **Agency** and **Bibliophage**, through **Grammar** and **Handwriting**, to **Wordsmiths, Yacht** and **Zeal.** Look out for what she says about the word *yacht*!

Above all, the book is packed with practical, tried-and-tested ideas that are readily applicable in any primary setting. Every chapter is underpinned by a love of language and a passion to inspire children.

Roy Blatchford, series editor

INTRODUCTION

To teach or lead English in a primary school is simultaneously a privilege, a joy and a weighty responsibility. Shaping children's learning in the subject that is the cornerstone of the primary curriculum, the gateway to all learning, is no mean feat.

Where do you begin? What do you prioritise? And, crucially, how far do your own preferences and interests influence the design of that learning?

I felt similarly blessed and challenged when I was asked to write this book. The subject is so multi-faceted and encompasses such a broad field that it might well have filled several volumes. And how might one distil an ocean of information into 26 neat chapters when the themes are overlapping and interconnected?

Here I was fortunate – my editor gave me agency to shape this book to my own design and so I have made the most of those overlaps. But it got me thinking: how far do leaders, teachers and pupils have agency when it comes to English teaching and learning in UK primary schools?

The chapters of this book detail aspects of English that I believe are fundamental to successful outcomes. The suggestions all sit within the boundaries of a national primary English curriculum but are not directly lifted from it. In an education career spanning four decades, I always strove to deliver according to governmental, regional and school-level requirements, yet I found my *voice* and exercised *choice* within those boundaries.

That is how I have maintained my engagement and passion for teaching – my zeal.

Wonderful things can happen when teachers take greater ownership of the craft of English teaching, when children are empowered to take greater responsibility for their education, and as both sides see the impact of their decisions and actions. These themes are a thread that runs through the book, as it seems natural to me that Agency at the beginning leads to Zeal at the end of our journey together.

Michelle Nicholson

AGENCY

Tell me and I forget. Teach me and I remember. Involve me and I learn.

Benjamin Franklin

At 88 pages long, the current national curriculum for primary English (Department for Education, 2013a) is a weighty document. And that might be expected with that ocean of information to navigate. It's worth noting that, by contrast, the entire secondary national curriculum stands at 105 pages; the English section is 26 pages long and much of it merely requires that pupils build on primary expectations.

On a first read, the primary English curriculum might appear overly prescriptive; it directs you quite precisely as to when information should be drip-fed to pupils. It prescribes which spellings should be learned and when, at what point specific aspects of grammar and punctuation should be introduced, and gives detailed guidance surrounding reading skills, composition and even spoken language.

Currently, academies and private schools may choose not to follow the 2014 primary English curriculum, but all schools are required to offer a broad and balanced curriculum that must naturally include detailed provision for a programme of study for English. The likelihood is that once enough detail has been added for teachers to understand what is expected of them and their pupils, all schools would end up with a similar document. This is because 'the what, the when and the why' are all crucial in the teaching of English so that pupils learn the skills at an appropriate time and in a logical order.

Order generally begets consistency and rigour, which, in turn, surely begets good results. Conversely, everyone doing what they like, whenever they like, increases the likelihood of repetition, omission, confusion. At its loosest, this approach mimics the haphazard era of my own primary education in the 1970s. But this was also known as a time of academic freedom and agency; behind every whim of lesson or topic was an interest, a passion and a desire to inspire learners.

I began teaching as the 1980s gave way to the 1990s, a time when the first concept of a centralised curriculum was appearing in the guise of lorries delivering boxes of ring-bound programmes of study. Despite the aim of standardisation, there was still a lot of choice in curriculum design and delivery. There was a sense of 'freedom within a framework', even if certain topics didn't make the cut.

It can often feel as though the tightness of modern school curricula has squeezed out any element of choice and voice. How far can teachers be flexible in their own lesson design within a school framework? How can you ensure you bring your own personality to an inherited lesson? There is more room for this than we might initially think.

English as a subject is broad and beautiful. And the thing about the national curriculum is that it may detail the 'what' and the 'when' as well as a bit of the 'why', but not the 'who' nor yet the 'how'.

The English national curriculum is merely a package of information: schools choose the box to put it in and teachers can choose the wrapping, ribbons and the pizazz with which to deliver it. Wise advice to any teacher using a scheme who is worried about making any adaptation for learning: fidelity doesn't mean rigidity. Let your personality shine through, allow yourself the freedom to put your own spin on lessons, introduce the pupils to books you love and lessons they will remember. Share ideas to bring the subject matter alive and handy tips to help them learn. Think about what works when and for whom. Reflect on what doesn't work and why. Embrace your knowledge and leverage your agency to make adjustments and enhancements that give your teaching impact.

PUPIL AGENCY

If we accept that involving pupils in decisions is a positive thing, how far should we allow pupils to have a voice and a choice in their learning? Does the curriculum make children believe they are players rather than pawns?

Fostering agency in primary school children is essential for their development as independent, self-motivated learners. Examine your English curriculum with that in mind and consider the extent to which it gives pupils the ability to act autonomously in their own learning and decision-making processes.

READING

As pupils progress through their schooling, they encounter varying levels of choice when it comes to reading material. From careful curation of phonically decodable scheme books, through teacher choice of the end-of-day class read, all the way to the A-level English Literature syllabus, it does appear that young people have a lot of their reading decisions mapped out for them. Alongside prescribed texts, pupils should be encouraged to select books for their own enjoyment and, as far as possible, should have free rein in that choice.

The choice element should come first. If we engage our readers and introduce them to the joy of reading, there is more of a chance that they will become readers: the will provides motivation to acquire the skill.

An important aspect of choice is that a reader has the right to change their mind about a book they have chosen to read. We've all picked up a book that just isn't quite hitting the mark for us and that we have no inclination to finish. Children are no different. Surely we all have the right to choose which books we reject as well as select. Allowing pupils that freedom is an important way of saying, 'I trust your judgement; it is valid.' Similarly, there might be times when pupils want to read the same book over and over or read a book that is 'far too easy for them'.

In 1992, the author Daniel Pennac (latest edition, 2006) listed these points as part of his 10 incontrovertible 'rights of the reader' published in his book of the same name.

WRITING

We can consider writing similarly, especially bearing in mind the key drivers for getting pen to paper. In 2011, Dr Jeni Smith devised a mirror list of 'rights of the writer' (see Section Two).

Choice and voice play a key part in motivation for writing. Again, if we look at the early years in school, we encourage exploratory play and independent learning that is child-centred and initiated by a pupil's interests and needs. We then seem to spend the following years reversing that approach by providing less and less autonomy and choice, especially when it comes to writing. Researchers such as Ross Young and Felicity Ferguson regularly cite an exact correlation between motivation and the ability to see oneself as an authentic writer with agency.

A clue to the regard both pupils and adults in school have for writing lies in the oft-used term 'work' to describe writing-based activities. Pupils are told to 'get on with your work'; in return, they tell you when they have 'finished their work' or 'handed their work in'. To my mind, the terms 'work' and 'pleasure' rarely go hand in hand. It stands to reason that students who have a say in their learning are more likely to be engaged and motivated and perhaps less likely to view it as a task for production and consumption within the confines of the classroom.

A simple tweak can be to encourage pupils to be involved in decisions around their writing. Rather than everyone working on a biography on a person chosen by the teacher and writing it up in their books for the sole readership of their teacher, for example, we can let pupils decide about whom they will write, how they will present the information and who their audience will be.

Volitional writing is more achievable when pupils are given opportunities for authentic writing experiences and can develop their own identity as a writer. Rather than writing letters to imaginary creatures or stories that only the teacher will ever read, engineer lessons in which pupils write about what matters to them, for audiences that matter to them. Children will naturally begin to see their validity as writers, take pride and pleasure in writing and grow in confidence and skill as a result.

> ## ASIDE
>
> Here are 10 easy-to-adopt strategies that can help pupils develop a strong sense of agency and bring personal as well as academic benefits:
>
> 1. Collaborative projects: Provide opportunities for pupils to choose whom to work with on a written project or group presentation. Encourage students to explore topics of interest to them, and allow them to decide what to produce and how to present it.
> 2. Peer teaching: This could take the form of coaching a classmate on a spelling strategy that has helped them or giving them feedback on something they have written. Perhaps an older pupil could choose a book to read to a group of younger pupils in the library at lunchtime.
> 3. Self-run discussion groups: These could be on a subject of their choosing, but with older children, book talk discussions are perfect for developing reading comprehension. Pupils can even take turns to have roles within the group in the style of reciprocal reading.
> 4. Class book choice: A simple, but not always adopted, idea is to give pupils a genuine say over the class book. From the very youngest pupils voting for one of three books on offer at the end of the day, to older students researching and presenting on possible candidates for the next class read, this is an impactful way of handing over agency to a class.
> 5. Personal book choice: Whether pupils are working through a scheme of phonically decodable books or texts graded by Lexile rating[1], it is always good to give children the opportunity to take home a book of their own choice. Whether it is a story an adult might read to them or a non-fiction book that they will explore alone by looking at the pictures, this is a vital aspect of reading motivation.

---

1   Lexile rating or (lexile measure) is a standardised numerical score based on word complexity and sentence structure that indicates the level of reading difficulty of a given text.

6. Invite pupils to decide how to write up information in subjects beyond the English curriculum: They may choose to share what they know about the Mayans in the form of a letter, diary, report or graphic organiser, for example.
7. Empower choice through skill building: Explain the function of aspects of grammar and teach ambitious vocabulary so that pupils can choose which words and language structures will shape their oral and written sentences for best impact on their reader.
8. Freedom within a framework: Rather than structuring writing lessons so that each outcome ends up being a carbon copy of the teacher's example, show pupils how to craft their own writing that they frame around a theme of their own choosing.
9. Writing for others: Allow pupils to choose the audience for their writing. Who are they communicating to and how do they want their reader to react?
10. Writing for personal consumption: Provide writing journals to allow pupils the time, space and privacy to express themselves in writing without agenda or judgement.

BIBLIOPHAGE

To read a book for the first time is to make an acquaintance with a new friend. To read it for a second time is to meet an old one.

Chinese proverb

Taken from the Greek language, the word *bibliophage* describes someone who metaphorically devours books in their passion to read them: a bookworm.

Booklovers are revered in educational circles; a child who loves to read is surely on a good trajectory for learning. If you love reading, you'll do it more and get better at it. If you're getting good at reading, you'll enjoy it and do it more.

Time and time again, studies highlight the link between reading for pleasure and academic success. We know that well-read children become stronger writers, broadening their vocabulary and cultural understanding, and generally raising their attainment across the curriculum. So, we have myriad reasons for raising the profile of reading in school. But how do we get children into that virtuous cycle of practice, proficiency and pleasure?

The current primary English national curriculum puts 'reading for pleasure' firmly on the agenda, mentioning it frequently and even making the lyrical claim that reading, 'opens up a treasure-house of wonder and joy for curious young minds' (Department for Education, 2013a).

Most schools are now attuned to this and there has certainly been a growing involvement in the Reading for Pleasure campaigns led by Teresa Cremin at the Open University, for example. Nonetheless, the National Literacy Trust's annual surveys report an alarming decline in the numbers of children who declare reading to be a pleasurable activity (2024a, 2024b). The most recent report reveals that these figures are at an all-time low.

As well as instructing children in *how* to read and giving them the 'skill' to progress, we must also instil the 'will' to pick up books freely. There are endless activities and gimmicks that can be introduced into school to inspire reading, from Get Caught Reading campaigns to book fairs and author visits. These activities can reignite a love of reading in children who then go home to a bedtime story or those who have a shelf full of books that they used to enjoy. But are these strategies enough to develop robust reading habits in children who are resistant to the charms of great literature?

As scholar and author Maryanne Wolf (2008) wrote: 'We know that emotional engagement is the tipping point between leaping into the reading life or remaining in a childhood bog where reading is endured only as a means to other ends.'

TECHNOLOGY: A DISTRACTION OR ATTRACTION

Children don't always choose to read at home; it is a perennial problem. Over a decade ago, a survey by the National Trust (2013) discovered: 'More than half (54% of children surveyed) prefer watching TV to reading.' We live in a visual age where interactive content can be more appealing than reading a book. Today, with the prevalence of screens, it's no wonder that adults and children alike turn their attention away from reading as a pastime.

Hungarian psychologist Mihaly Csikszentmihalyi (2008) identified and hypothesised about an experience that he termed 'flow'. He defined it as 'a state in which people are so involved in an activity that nothing else seems to matter'. For an activity to induce intense enjoyment to the point of total absorption, it needs to provide enough challenge to stimulate the brain and stave off boredom, but not so much that the person becomes frustrated and opts out. That's what getting lost in a book is all about, but, unfortunately, video games are designed to induce that state more readily.

Even toddlers seem to understand how to navigate an interactive screen these days. But perhaps rather than throw our hands in the air, we need to get better at harnessing technology and using it to our advantage. Video games, TV programmes and even online clips all have a subtitle facility. A recent campaign, Turn on the Subtitles, by the advocacy group of the same name, made the bold claim that by doing so, parents and carers might double the chance of their children becoming proficient readers.

And, of course, many reading schemes have online versions of their books from early decodable texts to follow along with, so digital media is certainly here to stay.

TIME FOR READING

Putting the lure of the screen aside, there are many other activities competing for the attention of the modern child. Many have busy schedules filled with extracurricular activities, sports and social events. Some enjoy meeting up with friends, while others may have caring responsibilities or spend time between families.

Care givers are often all-too-guiltily aware of the need to develop children's reading skills, but perhaps not as cognisant of the bonding experience of sharing book time together. Video games or television can be *too* visually stimulating at times, whereas reading can de-stress the mind and engender a state of relaxation. However, if the very act of reading causes stress in itself – or a parent does not have the time or the skill to read well – there is another way in.

Consider buying audio versions of books so that children can get hooked on books that are age appropriate even if they are not read *to* by an adult at home. Audio versions will allow developing readers to hear language and stories that they cannot yet read but their peers can; books that are appropriate to their age and interest level. Otherwise, there is a danger that by the time some children can read a book, the content will feel too immature.

Audiobooks can be readily incorporated into a busy day to become the soundtrack to long journeys, part of a bedtime routine or part of a quiet visit to the school library. Yes, we do need to develop children's reading skills alongside the use of audiobooks, but the tradition of oral storytelling is far longer established than that of reading. Hooking children into the content is a sure-fire way of providing a reason to want to read independently.

BEGIN EARLY

Long before children are ready to read, we need to engender a thirst for literature. They need to feel books, turn the pages, enjoy the pictures, talk about what they have heard and begin to absorb the structures and conventions of literature.

Once in school, teachers have a race against time to support pupils to develop the will as well as the skill to read. But the crowded primary school curriculum means that time for reading can seem even further squeezed.

Preserve time for reading to pupils in school at all costs. No matter what age, children deserve the opportunity to hear books being brought alive by expert readers and experience the joy of listening to a great piece of literature as part of a community.

ROLE MODELS

The National Literacy Trust statistics (2024a) consistently cite positive reinforcement from family and friends and having reading role models as the biggest influence on children's reading frequency and enjoyment.

Yet we cannot assume that there will be someone in any home who can support an early reader with the mechanics of decoding. We cannot assume that there will be access to books, either owned or borrowed. And we cannot assume that there will be anyone at home who is modelling any positive reading behaviours. Of course, economically disadvantaged households do not automatically equate to households lacking in love for reading. Equally, while most parents and carers will recognise the value of reading to their young children, time constraints and pressures affect families regardless of economic background. Over the last five years, the National Literacy Trust has explored trends in parental reading to young children, and 2024 data taken from a survey of over 2000 respondents shows that only 50.5% of children under five were read to daily (2024c). (This figure is 15.1 percentage points lower than the equivalent survey in 2019.)

No matter what we put in place to encourage and support, many children only experience reading in the classroom. Fortunately, role models can take the guise of peers as well as adults. Factor in time for book discussions and recommendations and ensure that pupils see and hear people around the school modelling the reading behaviours that are promoted.

Look beyond the classroom: a Year 6 pupil could host a reading session for younger children in the library at lunchtime, for example. Older students could buddy up with younger pupils to support their reading; this can have a huge impact on the self-esteem and reading attainment of both parties.

BOOK CONNOISSEURS

Even when children want to read, the range of books available can be overwhelming. If you have pupils who find it hard to commit to a book and continually ask to change their choice, you might like to make browsing part of the regular reading diet. An effective way of doing this is through 'book-tasting' sessions, whereby a table can 'sample' a few books laid out as possible recommendations. At the end, they have a choice: they can either take a book away to continue reading it, make a note of one or two books that they would like to read in future or decide that none of these books are for them.

Where time is precious and engagement is crucial, there is no place for lacklustre literature; every book needs to earn its place in the reading curriculum. Choose books for their literary merit, not because they fit a topic or have a celebrity author. If pupils are steered towards quality books, there is a better chance that they will have a positive experience.

Consider building a core spine of books that you want pupils to encounter during their time in your school. These should be books and authors that all children ought to experience. Publish details on the school website so that parents and carers, as well as pupils themselves, are aware of the texts that form the backbone of their own personal reading besides those that they will be introduced to during reading instruction and read-alouds.

A love of a good book can build concentration in minds plagued with distractions and cravings for instant gratification. It can provide escapism and relaxation in stressful and difficult times. And, of course, it can pave the way for empathy and tolerance that is so crucial in today's world. This, then, is the holy grail of teaching: the trinity of the skill and the will that leads to the thrill of reading.

> ## ASIDE
>
> Reading should not be presented to children as a chore or duty. It should be offered to them as a precious gift.
>
> Kate DiCamillo
>
> Rewards for reading? Yes, pupils *could* earn points, marbles or small rewards for completing books or reading at home with an adult. Extra credit *could* be given to a pupil when another child completes a book that the pupil recommended to them. However, extrinsic motivators suggest that children are completing a task – perhaps something unpleasant or difficult – and need to be congratulated for having done so.
>
> In an article for *Primary Matters* magazine, Teresa Cremin (2019) suggests that: 'Reading for pleasure is more closely associated with intrinsic motivation; it is reading that children do for themselves at their own pace, with whom they choose and in their own way.' Look to build in social, emotional and cultural motivators for reading. If there is a positive ethos of reading in school, with pupils seeing being able to 'drop everything and read' as a goal and a privilege, they should move towards volitional reading, even when they still find decoding a challenge.
>
> Once a child builds enough fluency and stamina to read through an authentic text (not a dull decodable scheme book, but a story or article designed to open that 'treasure-house of wonder and joy'), they cease to require an incentive or compensation. For those who have discovered the idea that a book might have something interesting to impart, reading provides its own intrinsic rewards.

CRAFT

My responsibility as a writer is to be as good as I can be at my craft. So I study my craft … . Learning the craft, understanding what language can do, gaining control of the language, enables one to make people weep, make them laugh, even make them go to war.

Maya Angelou

Crafting any sort of writing is a challenging process. There are many separate and various skills that go under the banner of composition and transcription.

A novice writer needs to concurrently form letters correctly, spell words accurately, construct sentences logically and weave it all together creatively. To some, this might feel akin to riding a unicycle while juggling and singing. Writing skills and knowledge need to be applied across five different stages of a process: planning, drafting, revising, editing and publishing. The writer needs to have the big picture in mind, just as a master chess player does. Add a chess game into the unicycle mix and it is no wonder that children can feel utterly overwhelmed when it comes to putting pen to paper.

Furthermore, children often lack the stamina to write at length and their texts lack cohesion. For children with difficulties in any, or all, of these areas, independently written outcomes are consequently bland, fragmented and lacking in accuracy. Is it any wonder that enjoyment of writing is a casualty for many of our pupils? It is difficult to find enjoyment in a task that feels laborious and leads to unsatisfying results.

AUDIENCE AND PURPOSE

The average primary child cannot project themselves into a future in which writing skills will be needed for a GCSE examination, university application or job completion. While many children declare their desire to become professional footballers, very few children imagine a life as an author or even see that writing is a skill for life.

If a child doesn't see writing as a task to be valued in the here and now, we have little chance of helping them see a future with writing at the centre. The need for promoting a life-long love of reading is well documented – and indeed the national curriculum insists we nurture that – but do we ever consider how to ensure that children acquire a life-long positivity towards writing?

Giving pupils a reason to write – and someone to write for – can support effective writing and provide opportunities to teach pupils how to adapt their writing for different audiences and purposes.

Surely if a child is going to the bother of writing a letter of persuasion or complaint, they ought to have a genuine audience and something to gain from the effort. Do some research and work out which authors might reply personally, which local councillors are amenable to being contacted and which sports personalities have secretaries responsible for responding to fans.

Children need to know their target audience. As far as possible, design final written outcomes to have a genuine rationale to answer the questions 'Why am I writing?' and 'Who will see my work?' You may have noticed that children often take extra care with their handwriting when they are writing for an audience. Here are a few twists on familiar activities that might give more of a sense of purpose:

- Stories can be written with a specific audience in mind. They could be written to be shared with younger classes or to become part of a short story collection for the class book corner. Consider entering your class for competitions such as the BBC's 500 Words competition (www.bbc.co.uk/teach/500-words).

- Sports reports can be uploaded onto the school website or stored in a season's fixtures book with photos. Similarly, recountings of trips can be designed to be shared.
- School information letters can become direct messages to friends and family, including invitations to parents' evenings or assemblies or book recommendations created to give directly to a peer. When an appeal comes directly from the child, it tends to have a higher success rate.
- Pupils can write messages for their peers to be used as labels around the Early Years environment. Messages could include: *Wash your hands, Don't touch my model, Welcome to my café.*

READING

You may have noticed that, in many cases, underachieving writers do not read extensively. They therefore lack the ability to compose writing with a clear audience and purpose, drawing independently on what has been read. Instead, writing is characterised by an over-reliance on shoehorned aspects of taught grammar; it may have little or too much detail, be repetitive or lack cohesion.

It is generally accepted that to write in a literary way, children must have exposure to quality literature. Most school writing programmes use books as a model and ignition to subsequent writing. However, one might argue that the interconnectedness of books and children's writing is just as much about choosing books for their power to engage children with reading as it is to inspire their writing.

One of the great privileges of working in primary education is that you witness the emergence of young children's writing and observe as they find their own writer's voice. A child who has learned to manipulate their reader, entertain them or provoke a reaction has surely been acquiring those skills from their reading diet.

Reading different types of texts ensures that children become familiar with various styles of writing. Through this, they assimilate the tricks of the trade that a good writer uses to engage their reader. But is it as simple as that? Is it a form of osmosis whereby a student can unwittingly absorb the genius of a writer and automatically replicate the process?

The truth is that few children magically leap from reading into writing. So how can teachers support the reading-into-writing connection and help transfer what pupils are observing in terms of how words are used and spelled, and how words combine, into making their own writing powerful and engaging?

Modelling a writer's voice to help pupils find their own

Each stage of writing needs to be modelled to demonstrate the process, whether that be the ideation stage, planning, composing sentences or pulling everything together. Most writing schemes expose children to a range of quality literature with the aim of showcasing what good writers do to engage their readers. But rather than being able to mimic the style of specific authors and/or replicating the content of their work, we are teaching pupils the common features of writing and pointing out what the writers have done.

When reading with pupils in class, we can identify and explore these features and then follow up in writing lessons, by constructing a written model based on what the pupils have read and showing them in real time the process behind the writer's craft.

Vocabulary and language development

The more children read, the more words they encounter. This exposure helps them understand the meaning and usage of words in context. It stands to reason that children who read a broad range of books are likely to come across myriad words that they may not encounter in everyday conversation.

Moreover, reading helps children to understand the nuances of language. They learn about the synonyms, antonyms, idiomatic expressions and figures of speech that enhance our language. These all become part of their mental lexicon, and so when it comes time for writing, they have a broader selection of words to choose from. This allows them to express their ideas more precisely and creatively.

Sentence structure and grammar

Reading exposes children to different ways of constructing sentences. As they engage with books, they see examples of how sentences can be structured to convey meaning effectively. They should be supported to notice how authors use punctuation, vary sentence length and combine clauses to create rhythm and flow.

The national curriculum (DfE, 2013b) starts mentioning the correlation between reading and writing from Year 1, where it explains that when teachers make explicit reference to sentence structures in books: 'In due course, they (children) will be able to draw on such grammar in their own writing.'

Narrative flow and organisation

While vocabulary and grammar are important, a good writer needs to mix those ingredients effectively to pull together a cohesive and engaging text. When children read widely, they learn how different genres handle pacing and structure. They encounter clear examples of how to develop a beginning, middle and end of a tale. They see how authors introduce characters, build tension or conflict and resolve the story in a satisfying way. They also pick up on how to make a story engaging from the first sentence and how to keep the reader interested throughout the piece.

Similarly, through reading non-fiction, children observe how to build an effective argument or to explain a process clearly. This knowledge helps them to become more effective storytellers and essay writers.

Inspiration and creativity

Writers can usually only write about what they know and have experienced, either directly or indirectly. Reading adds to a young child's life experiences and knowledge and helps to develop empathy.

Exposure to new worlds, ideas and perspectives opens up creative possibilities for a child's own writing. Reading sparks a child's imagination and creativity, both of which are crucial for developing a unique voice in writing. The more they read, the more they can draw upon diverse ideas and experiences when crafting their own writing.

Choice and voice

It is a given that a book that happens to set my heart thumping may leave yours unmoved; a writing task that gets your creative juices flowing may leave mine stagnant and cold. We are not all the same; children have different cultural references, home experiences and interests and yet we expect them to spend many hours together applied in the same tasks.

From the outset, children need to know that their voice is worth being heard and that writing is a way of using their voice. As pupils begin mark-making, adults often scaffold what the child wants to tell people; however, it is important that we don't squash that voice by restricting choice. Examine planning to see whether an element of choice could be introduced in written tasks. Perhaps pupils could be liberated to follow their own interests within the boundaries of the lesson objectives.

Recently, I read 29 biographies of the same historical figure. Could the same skills have been rehearsed if pupils had been allowed to select their favourite athlete or singer to write about? In the past, I have taught pupils who would only put pen to paper if they were allowed to write about trains, Disney or Minecraft. It's always possible to find a way to make that work, if it means the pupil is engaged with the task.

Some language skills lend themselves perfectly to a particular text type, so we should ensure that pupils experience a mix of genres. Decide whether the purpose is to entertain, inform, persuade or argue, and consider whether that purpose could be achieved through a slightly different medium. For example, does it matter whether pupils record their fictional recounting as a letter or a diary entry? Could the students choose to present their facts on rainforest conservation as a newspaper report or an information leaflet, as long as they demonstrate the sentence structures, vocabulary and spellings that you have modelled? A teaching sequence remains vital, but accommodating individual interests fosters motivation and engagement.

Children should be shown that writing is valued and purposeful. They should see that writing can get results and that the skills they rehearse in English lessons can be used across the curriculum. They should also be given the satisfaction of seeing their writing out in the world; to know that there was a reason behind the effort. Ultimately, what we want is for pupils to develop a joy of writing and realise the power they have at their fingertips if they write well. A realisation that could give them a buzz so electrifying that they might be inspired to keep at it beyond the lesson.

ASIDE

Finally, it is worth asking yourself: are the pupils ever free to just write unhindered, or is every journey of pen on paper accompanied by the baggage of learning objectives, success criteria and 'next-step marking'? While the aforementioned are essential to improving the quality of writing, they can stifle creativity and willingness to commit.

To use another analogy: swimming lessons are necessary to perfect the skill and prevent drowning, but once you have mastered the basics, it's delicious to have some unstructured time to splash around and do whatever you please without an instructor critiquing your breathing technique.

Not all children will choose to write at home, so it's worth taking a leaf out of the Foundation Stage book and carving out some slots in a term for 'free writing', just as we would offer 'free reading' or a 'fun swim'. The best way to encourage a love for writing is by having fun with it so that developing skills is always a pleasure and never a chore.

DECODING

> To learn to read is to light a fire; every syllable that is spelled out is a spark.
>
> Victor Hugo

The national curriculum is designed to ensure that all pupils become confident, fluent readers so that by the time they leave the primary phase, they have attained sufficient reading skills to access texts from across the curriculum independently.

Before they can begin with word reading, children need to become familiar with handling books and turning pages (rather than swiping screens), and be guided to orientate text on a page. They will need support to recognise that print has meaning and corresponds to spoken sounds and words; to understand that the written word is a means of communication, just like talking.

Decoding is the seemingly basic skill of converting printed letters into spoken language; the ability to crack the cipher. For the last 20 years, systematic synthetic phonics (SSP) has been the prescribed approach in the UK. Early readers will initially be taught the one-to-one correspondence of a grapheme (the smallest unit of writing) to a phoneme (the smallest unit of speech sound). They then learn to synthesise groups of letters together to build words. And they need plenty of opportunities to repeat this until the learning is cemented.

As soon as pupils have been taught a handful of letter–sound correspondences and shown how they can be put together, they need to be given decodable books that allow them to apply their skills in context.

The sequence of reading books used in schools should adhere to the same progression in phonics knowledge as the school's phonics programme.

For their independent reading, pupils should have a decodable book that is perfectly matched to their current reading attainment (in addition to ones they may choose for browsing or being read to).

Phonological awareness combined with an understanding of the alphabetic system, when sufficiently rehearsed, leads to greater accuracy and a growing recognition of words 'on sight'. The idea is that pupils progress swiftly through the code. On the way, they learn to scoop up words into slightly larger chunks for efficiency: the regularity of adjacent consonants reducing the need to overtly blend; affixes such as -ing, -ed or un- being recognised and added to a blended root; morphemic syllables separated into clear blocks such as 'sand/pit'.

Gradually they will rely less on building words from their constituent parts and more on a familiarity with words they can read at a glance. As word reading skills become more automatic, pupils' cognitive load is freed up to focus more on comprehension of the text.

That is the theory. In practice, there will always be pupils who present with a barrier to reading, whether that be a barrier of opportunity or specific neurological difficulties. Early identification of pupils who are at risk of falling behind is vital. In most cases, quality-first teaching ensures that pupils' needs are met by expert practitioners skilled at adapting the content to reach the entire audience and making sure all pupils are busy and always included.

There is an expectation that all pupils will be taught through daily, discrete phonics sessions, building in length, from Reception onwards. In addition, practitioners should provide increasing opportunities for pupils to apply that burgeoning knowledge through:

- guided reading sessions that scaffold the new learning while giving an opportunity to rehearse the familiar
- dictations that support encoding and provide the opportunity to construct words in the context of sentences
- responding to signs and captions around the class.

KEEP UP, CATCH UP

Synthetic phonics is generally considered the best way of ensuring all pupils succeed in reading, and so the advice from the Department for Education (DfE) is that all pupils should be taught using this methodology. Research supports the view that only a minority of pupils with complex learning needs would be unable to benefit from decoding using this method, and yet there are too many instances of pupils being withdrawn from phonics teaching in mainstream education.

Where pupils struggle to keep up, intervention may be needed. Judicious use of assessment should target the exact nature of the need, and careful monitoring of the intervention should identify whether the gap is closing at a rapid enough pace. The approach should still be phonics first, but the steps may need breaking down further, repeating often and to feature additional scaffolding.

Older pupils are particularly vulnerable to falling further behind if word reading is not secured early on. Staff in key stage (KS) 2 can be less familiar with phonics teaching, and because most pupils have moved on, strategies they have relied upon may not be used in class. Pay special attention to the following:

- Have decodable books that are aligned to the interest age of the pupil, to avoid issues with engagement and self-esteem.
- Provide daily opportunities for pupils to consolidate word reading skills with a skilled adult at instructional as well as practice levels.
- Monitor interventions to ensure they are targeted to exact gaps. Too often, pupils repeat learning whether they need to or not, especially when intervention is for a group rather than an individual.
- Ensure pupils don't always miss the lesson they love to prioritise reading. This can be demotivating. Conversely, don't remove them from a reading or spelling lesson or the gaps will get bigger. It's a timetabling nightmare, but a healthy balance must be struck.

Some pupils find it difficult to see that a series of distinct sounds can combine to make a whole word, no matter how many times you sweep under the letters or move the letters closer and closer. Unhelpful reading behaviours include pupils sounding out each grapheme of an unknown word and then not saying the word at the end, or sounding out every single letter, even when the word is known. If the final act of synthesis eludes a pupil, try the following techniques:

- Start with oral blending[2] of the word; let them hear it several times before looking at the word.
- Connected phonation: Scoop up the sounds as you go, adding each one in turn to build the whole word, such as *mmm > mmuuuu > muummm > mum* or *r > rai > rain*.
- Model reading words in a book by saying each sound and immediately returning to the beginning of the word to blend. Add in a finger swoosh under the word to emphasise the act.
- Read the blended word repeatedly. When they see this word repeated in the next sentence, can they read it on sight or do they try to segment and blend again?
- Ask pupils to write the word after reading it to reinforce the visual pattern.

ORAL FEEDBACK TO SUPPORT SELF-REGULATION

Self-regulation is a vital key to closing reading gaps for learners. Can they monitor their reading and address errors or are they reliant on adult support? Poor executive skills such as weak working memory, inability to plan or problem-solve and lack of self-monitoring can impact pupils' ability to develop effective decoding skills.

These strategies should be modelled to scaffold the desired learning behaviour. Build a pupil's self-belief and sense of what is going well alongside a growing awareness of what they need to improve. Enlist the process of 'praise, prompt, pause' to increase intrinsic motivation and engagement.

---

2   Teaching pupils to manipulate phonemes, initially through oral blending, is a vital stage of reading. When you observe pupils who are struggling to blend graphemes, they often have little concept of how to combine individual speech sounds into whole words. This is usually abandoned once pupils have moved on to reading, but most pupils benefit from continuing this skill whenever new grapheme–phoneme correspondences (GPCs) are introduced.

Some examples:

- 'Great how you're holding your own book; keep your eyes on the page, not me.' (If needed: 'Much better – now you're looking at the words to see what they say. Put your finger under the word you are going to read next.')
- 'That sounded good; you made one mistake on the page ... can you find and fix it?' (If needed: 'Yes, well done – it could be "mum" because it begins "m-u", but look again at the last bit.')
- 'That was very good blending, but you missed a word and so the sentence didn't make sense. Can you see which word?' ('Great. Now read it again and see if it makes sense this time.')

READING INTO WRITING

Systematic phonics instruction also underpins the mechanics of writing. Naturally, an approach designed to teach correspondence of sounds to letters underpins encoding as well as decoding; it's a belt-and-braces line of attack. As pupils begin to assimilate 'the code', they acquire the power to record their own writing that others can read; at first with phonetic plausibility and then, increasingly, with orthographical accuracy. The transcription of phonemes into graphemes builds the solid foundation of all spelling knowledge and is a vital component of decoding itself. The act of recording each grapheme (especially while saying it aloud) slows down the process of grapheme recognition and embeds the order in motor memory.

While SSP schemes do call for the rehearsal of phonics through encoding activities, this component of the teaching sequence tends to be rushed or overlooked altogether. True, the phonics screening check examines reading only and, yes, pupils' ability to encode accurately generally lags behind their decoding skills. But segmenting is the inverse operation of blending and, as such, the process provides a further opportunity for practice. When the two skills are rehearsed side by side, there is a greater chance of embedding both.

This can take the form of:

- quick writes on mini-whiteboards during the phonics session
- the teacher modelling taking words apart during a guided reading session

- pupils moving plastic letters into a phoneme frame
- dictations for focus on word building rather than composition
- modelling the use of sound charts and mats to support encoding.

APPLICATION ACROSS THE CLASSROOM AND THE LEARNING DAY

For pupils to make swift progress in decoding, phonics activities should be woven in throughout the day. Be imaginative!

- Pin single-letter signs around the class and then refer to them throughout the day. 'Go and stand under the sign that says "ssss".'
- Have a 'password of the day' on the classroom door that pupils can read aloud whenever they enter or exit. This is a great way of reinforcing common exception words. 'This week's password is "she": sh-ee, she.'
- Leave hoops with chalked letters in the outside provision. 'Jump into the hoop that has the letter "p" making "puh".'

Support pupils' application of the skills they have learned through guided reading-and-writing activities, decodable instructions and captions around the class, and plenty of opportunities to see the text of books being shared with them.

ASIDE

'FIDELITY'

Fidelity to a phonics programme is vital for consistency, rigour and pupils' progression in reading. The teaching sequence should be followed, the suggested progression adhered to, and resources should not be incorporated from other schemes. However, fidelity is to a scheme and not a publisher. Books from a variety of publishers can be used, if they follow the exact same phonics progression as the scheme being used.

A mismatch of approaches and lethal mutations are especially problematic for vulnerable learners

Rigid adherence to a programme, without making any adjustments to meet the learning needs of your pupils, is not what is intended by fidelity. Slow down where needed, add scaffolds, prompts and explanations that support all pupils to succeed in reading.

At times, you may hear the phrase 'fidelity to the scheme' used as an excuse for the absence of joy in early reading activities. If you look purely at the plan on paper, it does appear to be devoid of fun. But if you want to motivate and engage pupils, you will need to bring your passion and personality to a lesson. Above all, you need to inject fun.

This is not to propose a return to distracting games in the teaching sequence or the introduction of materials from other schemes, but some of the strategies that were previously used to good effect have been lost through fear of veering from the remit of the scheme. The following activities can be used with any scheme without detracting from the pace or progression of the learning:

- Having a puppet who learns alongside pupils and sometimes reads the word incorrectly, giving the teacher an opportunity to correct and repeat without implicating a pupil.
- Using a sing-song voice for instructions such as 'my turn, your turn' or inviting all the pupils to join in as you 'shuffle, shuffle, shuffle' the flashcards.
- Inviting pupils to blend a word using a whisper voice, a giant's voice, a robot voice.
- Using thumbs-up or jump-up responses for binary questions, for example, thumbs up if the 'ea' grapheme in these words is making an 'ee' sound like 'knead' and thumbs down if it's an 'eh' sound like 'bread'.
- Making a mistake sometimes as you read and allowing the pupils to correct you.

EDITING

To write is human, to edit is divine.

Stephen King

Writing is a complex, multi-faceted process. Successful composition requires pupils to be given time and space to consider their writing, and there are different aspects of this, each achieving different aims.

Broadly speaking, there are five stages to writing: planning, drafting, composing, editing and publishing. Of these components, editing seems to get the shortest shrift. This could be the result of time pressures at the end of a lesson or writing unit, a lack of confidence to teach this aspect of writing or a combination of both.

As educators, we have all come to understand the editing process to a degree. Whether it be cutting superfluous chunks from an undergraduate dissertation to make the word count, or carefully phrasing a pupil's end-of-year report to get the tone right and the message home, we have learned the craft of the rewrite. We employ that knowledge and skill when we review pupils' compositions and suggest 'improvements' on their behalf.

But how well do we transfer that competency to pupils so that they might independently evaluate and enhance their initial drafts? How do we move from implicit knowledge to explicit teaching?

By KS2, pupils know that editing and proofreading are necessary parts of the writing process. They can probably tell you that the *why* is to improve their writing, but I would argue that few have a clear understanding of the *how*.

Like all stages of the writing process, editing is a skill that needs to be taught and mastered. Simply requiring it – or having a special book or a different colour pen for it – doesn't automatically make it happen. Similarly, allocating time to editing doesn't automatically make it *effective*.

The 2014 curriculum explicitly mentions editing as a process and places the onus on the pupil to perform that task.

From Year 1 onwards, pupils need to be taught to re-read their writing to check that it makes sense! Editing writing combines two distinct processes: revising and proofreading. Editing can be taken to mean revisions that are made to enhance the quality of the writing, whereas proofreading is a subskill that focuses on the accuracy of a piece. The national curriculum gives a clear objective for each from Year 2 onwards: the goal is for all pupils to be able to evaluate the effectiveness of their own writing (and that of others), propose improvements and proofread for accuracy of punctuation and spelling.

MODEL AND SCAFFOLD

Established writers have a team of professionals to help them with evaluation; for our pupils, we need to help them internalise the act of revising, proofreading and evaluating. At the point of request, we need to consider what we want from the process as well as what we hope the pupils will get from it.

As with all aspects of teaching, modelling is crucial. If telling a pupil to edit their writing yields a blank look and little improvement, you may have to go back a step and show *how* that is performed and *what* they should be aiming for. Offer strategies for success and independence and, to avoid further overload in the already complex task of writing, introduce strategies separately and gradually build a repertoire. Use feedback judiciously to provide prompts; begin to reduce support as pupils become confident to use the strategies independently.

Encourage pupils to view composition as part of the writing journey rather than the destination. Show them examples of authors' first drafts so they see that editing is something all good writers have to do. Support them to unpick the types of edit and improvements that have been made:

additions, removals, moves, substitutions (ARMS). Can your pupils make these types of improvements? Encourage dialogue around this and an exploration of the writing process. Model examples and commentate upon the revisions as you make them (see examples in Section Two).

One simple scaffold is an editing checklist that pupils can use to help them improve any writing, whatever the subject. They should also refer to their success criteria as a guide; have they included everything they should to make this piece of writing effective? For KS1 pupils, a 'checking strip', like that shown below, might focus on simple proofing checks.

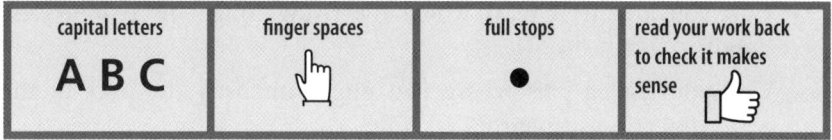

An example of a simple checking strip.

Provide the opportunity for pupils to discuss and evaluate their writing with peers and teachers at each stage: is my writing working for you as a reader? We respond as readers so pupils can see that edits are being made to better serve their audience. This removes some of the 'threat' that the concept of editing can bring, particularly when it is conflated with 'teacher marking and corrections'.

CONFERENCING

Editing for the sake of the reader rather than for one's own benefit is a huge distinction needed for all pupils but particularly for those who are reluctant to make any revisions to their writing. Children seem to fall into two groups: those who profess a dislike of writing, and – interestingly enough – those who are supremely confident in their writing prowess.

The struggling writer is likely to have been exhausted by the process and see revisions as a direct criticism that will lead to 'more work'. They find writing tricky anyway, so can find it difficult to spot how their composition could be improved or where the inaccuracies are. Furthermore, some take the suggestion that they might need to alter their work especially personally, so the conversation during adult-to-pupil verbal feedback (conferencing) needs to be managed very carefully.

At the other end of the scale, the overconfident writer can be resistant to change; they believe that what they have written is good (or even great) and they have been told so many times. They are unused to the need to make refinements to their writing and can be reluctant to start. This can be a barrier to moving into the greater depth standard.

The answer is to take the writing process back to purpose and audience, and support them to consider the needs of their reader: reframe feedback from 'How could you improve this sentence?' to ideas such as:

- How can you help the reader to visualise precisely what you mean?
- Can you identify a part where the reader might need more/less detail?
- Can you find a part where you might intensify the pace of the action/increase suspense?
- Look back at the success criteria with a partner and invite them to tell you which parts you could work on to make your writing more engaging for them.

Writing is a personal act; it necessitates revealing yourself and your skills to others. Being asked to make changes can feel like a judgement on ourselves, not just our skills. And it can be tricky to be objective about something you considered to be acceptable writing.

Another way of supporting is to model two different versions of your own writing and invite the pupils to evaluate each one. Which do they prefer and why? Help them to consider the effect of word order, for example:

Clumsily, he made his way upstairs in the dark.

He clumsily made his way upstairs in the dark.

Or vocabulary choice, such as:

Little Red Riding Hood

Little Crimson Riding Hood

Or sentence length or punctuation:

There was a loud rattle, a muffled scream and a thud that sounded like something huge hitting the floor; then darkness filled the room.

A loud rattle, a muffled scream and a thud. Then darkness.

Provide support specifically for editing in a guided group. When you hold conference with pupils, ensure that you first respond as a reader: How does the writing make you feel? Find a positive response to lead with. Which parts do you love? Which sections work well? Then help them focus on an area that might need more attention.

PEER FEEDBACK

In the same way, pupils can provide peer-to-peer feedback, although this should always be modelled first. Consider providing speaking frames that could scaffold their responses and make sure they provide meaningful – and kind – feedback:

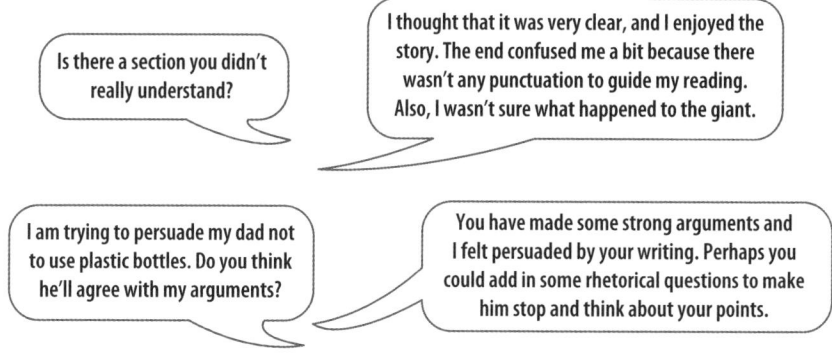

Peer-to-peer feedback.

PROOFREADING

It might be tempting to treat editing as one step, perhaps because of time pressures. However, there is little point in meticulously combing through a section of text, eliminating spelling errors or adding in missed punctuation, if that section might be removed from the final version. That said, editing as you go makes final proofing an easier task. It can be tricky to notice mistakes in a piece of extended writing. A good habit is to get used to checking for sense and accuracy sentence by sentence.

The pupils' mantra should be: 'Say the sentence, write the sentence, check the sentence.' Building in pit stops where you ask pupils to pause and read what they have written every 15 minutes or so (or whenever they reach the end of a paragraph) is a great way of encouraging pupils to monitor their writing as they go.

When we re-read our own writing (especially when the writing process was recent), our brain will often compensate for any mistakes, and we read what we intended to write. A way to avoid that error blindness is to allow pupils to practise on a piece of writing that isn't their own. This builds their understanding of how to approach the task effectively. There is an example of an activity that you could try in Section Two.

Pupils will also benefit from being given a narrow focus for proofreading rather than an open instruction to 'check your writing'. Give them something specific to look out for such as:

- finding six spellings that you want to check in the dictionary, or any 'non-negotiables' such as commonly used spellings/capitals for names
- looking at your verb endings to see whether you need to chop, change or double the last letter before adding 'ed'
- focusing on your own personal target
- spotting a class area of weakness, such as *your/you're*
- checking against a specific topic area, such as key words that all pupils will have included.

Teach pupils specific strategies that professional proofreaders use. For example, the tip below is easy to employ:

> This peace of riting has got lodes of seppling mistaiks. If we teech chidren to read the work backwads there is more chance of them spoting the errers as there not focusing on the context. It relly is a usefull trick to show your pupals. Howeva, they wont spot homophones or misused words as these are dependant on contest.

Despite giving pupils time and support to edit, you may still find that the end result isn't as effective as you had hoped. If so, take a step back and re-evaluate. What is the issue?

Children aren't sure what to look for:

- Model the process, commentating on how and why you are making revisions.
- Be specific rather than giving an open-ended instruction. What would you like the pupils to look for specifically?

Cognitive overload:

- Focus on a small area of the writing rather than the whole text.
- Focus on one skill at a time, perhaps through use of editing stations.

Too much time/too little time:

- Build in pit stops.
- Hold guided writing conferences for editing.

ASIDE

PUBLISHING

Publishing is integral to the editing process. Why bother refining writing at all if it doesn't have an audience? Not all writing needs to be edited. Some examples of pieces of writing that don't need editing could include a diary entry as a cathartic writing process, a journal as a solo exploration of ideas or even a list as an aide memoire. But if there is an intended readership beyond the writer, then the author has a duty to make it as engaging as possible.

Publication, whether that be a verbal or visual presentation, necessitates polishing. When the pupils have chosen an authentic audience for their writing, they will often be more motivated to ensure that the finished product is as good as it can be.

Perhaps encourage the pupils to think of the process as 'polish, proofread, publish'. The opportunity to share their complete masterpiece, and witness the effect on the reader or listener, leads to a final 'p', which is wonderful to behold in young writers: pride.

FLUENCY

So it is with children who learn to read fluently and well: They begin to take flight into whole new worlds as effortlessly as young birds take to the sky.

William James

Since the disruption of Covid-19, we annually see that fewer than 75% of pupils attain the nationally expected standard for reading in Year 6 (and, in truth, even before then it was never above 80%) ('Key stage 2 attainment: National headlines', DfE, 2024a). If one-quarter of the nation's 11-year-olds leave primary school without meeting the age-related expectations in reading, we can assume that in KS3 they might struggle to keep up with the disciplinary and substantive reading needed across the secondary curriculum.

More worryingly, these figures dip significantly for pupils classed as economically disadvantaged. If we are to close the attainment gap that grows between children experiencing financial hardship and their non-disadvantaged peers, and if we acknowledge that reading attainment is the key to this, we need to take responsibility for prioritising reading in schools.

FLUENCY AS A BRIDGE TO COMPREHENSION

Fluency, as a concept, has been traditionally underdeveloped in reading instruction in the UK. Until recently, the focus was on phonics over comprehension, and the feeling was that once pupils understood what they were reading, they would be able to read with greater fluency. While phonics knowledge is the key to the reading code, the ultimate prize is being informed, entertained and satisfied by what you have read.

The link between fluent reading and good comprehension has long been established. In the words of Maryanne Wolf, 'Fluency is the developmental process that connects decoding with everything we know about words to make the meaning of the text come to life. Fluency is a wonderful bridge to comprehension and to a life-long love of reading.'

If a read-aloud sounds monotone, staccato and the effort appears laboured, it is likely that the reader is struggling to derive any meaning from the text. With cognitive load taken up by the very act of decoding, there is little capacity for considering sense.

By contrast, a fluent reader effortlessly decodes, and their wide vocabulary knowledge enables them to scoop up word meaning as they go. A fluent read is smooth, well-paced, accurate and expressive. Automaticity of skills leaves the brain free to monitor content and process the meaning of phrases, sentences and the whole text. When a read-aloud *sounds* engaging, the likelihood is that the reader is comprehending as they read. A fluent reader has crossed that bridge.

FROM PHONICS TO FLUENCY

If phonics offers a foundation to reading, fluency is one of the pillars of reading instruction. For a pupil battling to blend word by word, the effort involved is huge; stamina, and any possible enjoyment, quickly wanes. Fluency creates an avalanche of reading skill and confidence, but it needs a catalyst. To transition from phonics to fluency, readers need to practise regularly and have the process explicitly modelled to them.

In early reading, fluency instruction involves strategies such as repeated reading of words to smooth out blending; scooping up of words into meaningful phrases; revisiting sections of texts to inject pace and prosody. All the while, these skills are modelled: 'Watch how I did that; listen again and then you try.'

In the process, pupils will begin to recognise more words on sight and build greater automaticity and fluidity as a result. It's important they realise that this is the aim. With decodable texts, the same words will tend to appear again and again. Nonetheless, some pupils approach them as though they have never seen them before, often stopping to blend a word they met in the previous sentence. Encourage them to spot those repeated words and expect to read them on sight. As reading mileage increases, pupils should build a growing repertoire of sight words.

Re-reading of texts is an easy-to-set-up activity for early readers. This could take the form of:

- a repeat group read of the previous day's guided reading text, this time focusing on a smooth, expressive read
- a paired re-read of a decodable book at a pitch that the pupil can access independently
- a re-read of a book that they have read before to build confidence before meeting a new text.

While pupils are developing blending skills, they will need multiple re-reads of their independent home-reading book before they change. If parents and carers are keen to swap before this has happened, prompt them to evaluate the read-aloud: did the child give a convincing read? If the answer is 'no', the likelihood is that the child will always be faced with books that feel just beyond fluency. While learning to blend unfamiliar words is vital, and learning through error is useful, there needs to be a 'just right' window of tolerance. A fluency-level reader needs:

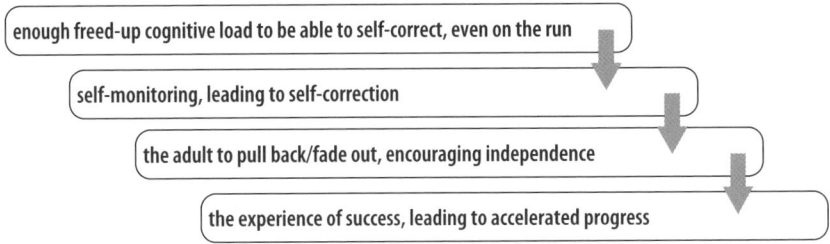

SPEED

As pupils blend new words more efficiently and recognise more words on sight, reading becomes less choppy and increases in pace. When the Teacher Assessment Frameworks were originally published in 2017 (Standards and Testing Agency, 2017 (updated 2024)), there was a suggestion that, for a child to be reading at the age-related standard, they should have a reading rate of 90 words per minute by the end of KS1. Whilst the DfE does not give official reading rates for the end of Y6, a notional reading rate of 150 words per minute is often cited.

The release of these figures prompted a wave of reading lessons with stopwatches at the ready. But if you did happen to time pupils' reading speed, you'd discover that 150 words per minute sounds natural to listen to on an age-appropriate text. It is not fast-paced skimming, nor barking at a text with purpose and without expression. This pace is a normal, pleasant talking rate.

The misunderstanding that fluency is about building speed persists. Tim Rasinski (2012) insists: 'In its fullest and most authentic sense, fluency is reading with and for meaning, and any instruction that focuses primarily on speed with minimal regard for meaning is wrong.' Fluency is not about reading fast; it's about reading fast *enough* to gain comprehension and enjoyment.

When reading aloud at this rate, the reader has time to inject dynamics of louder and quieter, and even to linger over the words that add weight to the meaning. Far from encouraging Year 6 pupils to speed up in their reading, you might find yourself reminding them to slow down, to add prosody (expressive reading), take in the meaning and convey it to the listener.

PROSODY

As pupils move through primary school, there is often less emphasis on reading aloud. The bedtime read by a parent often drops off, and even avid readers tend to squirrel themselves away to read privately. At school, the end-of-day read might be squeezed by time pressures, but it is vital that children continue to hear texts expertly modelled daily. As well as reading aloud, even the oldest pupils in school benefit from being read to.

It's all too easy for the brain to become passive during 'silent' reading. Have you ever been reading when tired and suddenly realised you've not taken anything in? Reading aloud forces readers to pay attention to accuracy as well as pace, pronunciation, intonation and expression. These factors are what build fluency, and a fluent read delivers meaning to the reader as well as the listener.

If fluency as an entire concept is a relatively recent focus in British education, the role of expressive reading as a vital strand of fluency was especially overlooked. Prosody has had growing attention in the last few years, due in no small part to interventions such as the Reading Fluency Project from the organisation HFL Education (also known as Herts for Learning). Details can be found at: www.hfleducation.org/reading-fluency.

A simple, small-group routine to develop pupils' prosody is to model an expert read, invite pairs of pupils to 'echo'[3] back small sections and then practise a longer section through repeated re-readings. Providing the opportunity for pupils to perform to a group provides motivation for children – auditory feedback of their own performance – and positive responses from peers – confirmation to the child that they are making progress.

FLUENCY MASTERY: DEEP AND WIDE

Fluency is not an end point or a stage of development; we can all be more fluent or less fluent depending on what we are reading. I struggle to sound convincing when I read aloud an unfamiliar Shakespeare text, and I might have to re-read a technical manual a few times to clarify my understanding. Conversely, I can give a wonderfully expressive performance of Michael Rosen's *We're Going on a Bear Hunt*, and I can whip through a 'beach read' in a couple of hours.

For dysfluent and fluent readers alike, practising reading – the act of reading, not of answering questions – remains key to building reading confidence across increasingly challenging texts.

Repeated reading, or deep reading, is a powerful technique proposed by S.J. Samuels. By reading the same text multiple times, readers become more familiar with the words and their patterns. This helps them to read more smoothly and confidently and, rather than perceiving it as boring, children derive motivation from the experience. This is undoubtedly

---

3   Use echo reading judiciously as a strategy. Asking the whole class to echo read can negate the purpose by resulting in a dreary chant that alienates confident readers and allows the pupils who need the practice to hide behind a mumble.

due to the affirmation they receive as they hear themselves performing noticeably better.

A direct consequence of this increased confidence (and undoubtedly the increased sight vocabulary that has developed) is the impact that Samuels (1979) noted on reading unseen texts: 'Repeated readings produce gains that extend to new material, suggesting that the method improves underlying processes that benefit overall reading fluency.'

Wide reading is also key. Pupils need to read a range of texts, on different themes, by varied authors. As children increase the amount they read, they repeatedly encounter the same words and phrases. This enables a swifter read, knowing what to expect and building comprehension across phrases: 'Once upon a *time*' or 'happily ever *after*'.

When seeking to extend pupils' reading mileage, short texts are invaluable: collections of stories, articles, self-contained chapters of a non-fiction book, poems and picture books. Consider the experience gained by moving from a funny story to a biographical text to a news article in one week. While the stamina needed to read through a novel over a term is valuable, there need to be regular opportunities for pupils to experience a complete story arc and see how a short report is structured. This is especially important for pupils who never seem to get to the end of a book.

As pupils become fluent readers, the resulting improvement in comprehension helps them discover the joy of reading. They realise that a well-written text can provoke a reaction of laughter, fascination, horror or even tears. Inspiration derived from discovering the joy of reading provides intrinsic motivation to read more and, before long, children have hopped onto the virtuous cycle of reading for pleasure.

ASIDE
ASSESSMENT

Fluency assessment needs to be a synthesis of information drawn from a pupil's read-aloud. Consider each element individually and then look at how each aspect impacts the pupil's understanding as a whole. Comprehension is the ultimate goal.

Speed: Time the child and assess the number of words they can read per minute on an age-related text. As we have ascertained, however, reading rate can also be assessed by simply listening to the pupil read and determining whether the pace sounds natural. The sweet spot is fast enough to maintain sense and clarity, and slow enough to maintain accuracy and not become garbled.

Prosody: This is assessed by monitoring how expressive a pupil's reading sounds and whether any due regard is paid to punctuation, dynamics and injecting meaning into the reading. Evaluate whether a child starts off with good expression and pace but then slows down and loses focus. A fluent reader sounds like they are understanding the text at the point of reading.

Accuracy: As you listen to the child read, keep a running record of the types of errors they are making. Are they:

- missing out words
- inserting extra words
- reversing words, e.g. *was/saw*
- mispronouncing words
- stopping at words they don't know and refusing to read them without prompting.

As with all assessment in English, use the information gained to adapt teaching and support pupils' improvement. Do pupils notice when they have made a mistake and self-correct, or do they plough on without addressing it? Knowing the areas for development allows for targeted support as well as working with a pupil to develop their strategies for metacognition in reading.

GRAMMAR

It's perfectly obvious that there is some genetic factor that distinguishes humans from other animals and that it is language-specific. The theory of that genetic component, whatever it turns out to be, is what is called universal grammar.

Noam Chomsky

The word *grammar* comes from a Greek term (*grammatikè téchnē*) that means 'art of letters'. Its meaning later diverged into two paths, the first of which honed the meaning to refer to the rules of writing. The second is the subject of debate, but some linguists believe that in the dark ages – where grammar pertained to the knowledge of the learned classes – the word evolved to form *glamour*.

It could be said that both definitions detract from the original ambition of the term: a means of describing the artistry of language and how we use words to convey meaning in the same way as we do in other art forms. The idea that grammar is purely about rules or is a mysterious skill privy only to the intelligentsia persists, along with the negative connotations these definitions bring.

As a result, the theme of grammar in primary education has attracted much debate and controversy, particularly over the last decade.

When the revised national curriculum for schools was released, there was much consternation in the primary sector over the sheer volume of the primary English section (DfE, 2013a). Of the 88 pages of content, over half comprise appendices to explain the breakdown of terminology, as well as spelling and grammar expectations. The rationale was explained thus:

The overarching aim for English in the national curriculum is to promote high standards of language and literacy by equipping pupils with a strong command of the spoken and written word.

To do so, schools need to ensure that pupils are supported to:

- 'acquire a wide vocabulary, an understanding of grammar and knowledge of linguistic conventions for reading, writing and spoken language'
- 'write clearly, accurately and coherently, adapting their language and style in and for a range of contexts, purposes and audiences'.

The detail behind these ambitions also caused alarm in some. Suddenly, a plethora of grammar guides for educators and children appeared, along with grammatical-subject-knowledge training sessions. Teachers professed their anxiety over 'never having been schooled in grammar as a child'.

Any good grammar guide or course should leave learners reassured that, while they might have begun with an uncertainty over relative clauses or conjunctions, they should not fear grammar. Much like the wizard in Oz, grammar experts possess no special powers. Their role is to reveal and clarify the code so teachers see that, like Dorothy, they had the power all along.

In essence, grammatical structures are the building blocks of our language. They are our tool for communication, and for establishing relationships, clarification and creativity of thought.

From birth, we begin assimilating this knowledge and clarify the rules and patterns of the language so that we understand and can be understood. For most of us, that schooling towards accuracy and consistency happens from the moment we start speaking. We listen and then we attempt to replicate the language structures. We might be gently steered in the right direction if we mistake the patterns or if we haven't yet mastered the irregularities. Consider the following conversation, typical of informal, inadvertent grammar schooling:

Adult: 'What did you do at nursery today?'

Child: 'I drawed picture and we goed outside.'

Adult: 'You <u>drew</u> a picture and <u>went</u> outside. Wow – that sounds fun!'

MASTERY

The 'art' of grammar is that subtle shift that learners acquire as they master the language and understand how to refine it for precision, cause and effect. As skilled communicators, we can perceive how our choice of language can manipulate a listener or a reader. Take the following command:

Take the bins out.

The syntax is accurate and the message is clear. But a speaker may soon realise that a little courtesy is needed to achieve the desired outcome, and might experiment with modifying the sentence structure a little, perhaps by adding an adverb:

Please take the bins out. or *Take the bins out, please.*

They might inject a further level of politeness by adding modal verbs and turning the demand into a request:

Please can you/could you/might you/will you take the bins out?

They could expand further by adding words and phrases that tell the listener how urgent the task is or why it needs to be done. At this point before articulation, a skilled practitioner would evaluate whether the extra detail and reasoning adds to or detracts from the impact of the message, or whether concision would be more effective.

Please could you take the bins out tomorrow morning because I'd like a lie-in?

Quick – take the bins out because the lorry is here!

SEQUENTIAL SKILL BUILDING

Much of our grammar learning is gleaned from verbal interactions, but we also osmose from reading or being read to. The following sentence, typical of story openings, contains an array of grammatical features including nouns, verbs (in the past tense), adjectives, (fronted) adverbials, prepositions, a relative clause and even the passive voice:

Once upon a time, there lived a little prince who was kept in a tower.

Few young story listeners would fail to understand the meaning of this sentence, despite the fact that it employs a literary style ('there lived a little prince') rather than following more conversational language patterns ('there was a little prince'). However, most pupils would probably struggle to compose a sentence like that for several years.

We could say that young pupils' receptive grammar tends to be ahead of their productive grammar. A primary teacher's job is to build pupils' receptive grammar through opportunities in listening and reading, while unpicking that knowledge in order for them to produce it in their speaking and writing.

The grammatical elements of the national curriculum are referenced explicitly to ensure that pupils are taught deliberately rather than being expected to learn by osmosis. Look at any primary school textbook from any era and you'll see that there was always an expectation that pupils should learn the grammatical skills that underpin their sentence structure. The difference now is that they are prescribed sequentially so that pupils are taught the relevant skills in a logical, systematic fashion rather than bumping into them randomly.

Furthermore, they are overtly named to give pupils the ability to discuss their learning using precise, technical vocabulary rather than vague, imprecise terms like 'joining' words or 'doing' words.

Teachers can support pupils with gaps by understanding how the skills set out in the curriculum build upon each other. For example, in Year 5, relative clauses are introduced. However, there should be a clear progression of grammatical knowledge to get to that point:

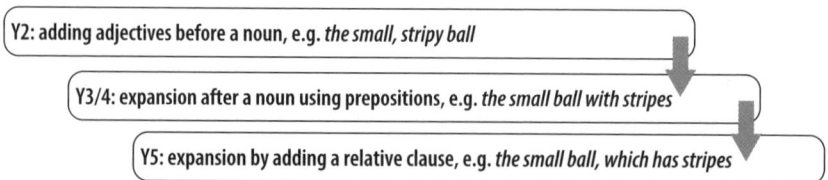

Y2: adding adjectives before a noun, e.g. *the small, stripy ball*

Y3/4: expansion after a noun using prepositions, e.g. *the small ball with stripes*

Y5: expansion by adding a relative clause, e.g. *the small ball, which has stripes*

This teacher knowledge is imperative for knowing which skills to revisit before introducing new, linked learning. It also better enables responsive teaching when gaps in prior learning are discovered. Problems with sentence structure often occur when pupils have not secured foundational learning before being asked to attempt more complex syntax.

Grammar expectations are deliberately pared back in Year 1. Allow it and don't push for complex structures that could confuse and disrupt the fluency of foundational writing skills. It is perfectly acceptable for pupils' written sentences to consist of a repetitive 'noun + verb' or 'noun + verb *and* noun + verb' pattern. Varying sentence structure and adding detail can come when the basic structure has been secured. As pupils hear and read more complex syntax, they will begin to experiment – first verbally and then in writing. Whenever pupils seem to be struggling, highlight the core of the sentence (who is doing what) and support them to build back up from there.

Grammatical understanding is not about learning functions of grammatical features in isolation, by rote or purely for purposes of identification in a test. Performing decontextualised grammar exercises offers little beyond a form of rehearsal and doesn't allow a pupil to see the purpose of selecting certain sentence structures within the context of a complete written or spoken piece.

Likewise, the naming of grammatical terms that often sparks controversy on social media is pointless at best if it serves no other purpose than to get pupils through a summative test at the end of Year 6. At worst, it can get in the way of learning and add confusion rather than clarity.

The real aim behind teaching linguistic terminology is to give pupils the tools to discuss grammar. It's not about the *what* but the *why*. Metalinguistic talk facilitates the exploration of compositional choices; the ability to analyse the effect the writer's language choice has on the reader. How does it affect understanding of a character, visualisation of a setting or following of the action? How does it affect your point of view? What devices were used to persuade you or convey information succinctly and clearly?

Pupils should explore authentic texts to see how authors employ language to manipulate their readers. Not so much magic tricks as 'tricks of the trade'.

Grammatical knowledge helps us to shape our language to give and receive messages more effectively – whether that be verbally or in writing – and should not, therefore, be knowledge restricted to a privileged few. With a modicum of understanding of the conventions behind the accurate and effective use of grammar, teachers can better support pupils' oracy, reading and writing skills. The ultimate aim is to show pupils how to make judicious choices and ensure grammar is the servant of their language and not the master.

> ## ASIDE
>
> Understanding of language structures drawn from examples in context gives pupils the power to use grammar effectively in their own writing. Myhill et al. (2016) define this as the ability to use 'grammar as choice', explaining that a solid pedagogy for writing should include 'explicit grammar teaching which draws attention to the linguistic choices and possibilities available to children and which has at its heart the creative shaping of text'. Try these ideas:
>
> - Model accurate sentence structure verbally and provide plenty of opportunity for oral rehearsal before asking pupils to write and use scaffolds to help frame new learning, for example, 'I like _____ but I don't like _____.' / 'Jozef was lonely because . . .'
> - Commentate your language choices as you model-write, for example, 'I am going to use a fronted adverbial here to set the scene: That night, she couldn't sleep.'
> - Remark on authorial choice of language structure as well as word choice as you read together, for example, 'Notice how the writer uses lots of short sentences here. What is the effect on us as we read? Can you spot any adverbs that tell us how the volcano is erupting?'

- Invite pupils to experiment with word order and evaluate what it does to the emphasis of a sentence as they read it aloud, for example:
    - <u>Silently</u>, he crept through the room.
    - He <u>silently</u> crept through the room.
    - He crept through the room <u>silently.</u>
- Support pupils to manipulate clause structure, order and length and consider the effect on the reader, for example:
    - As soon as they closed the door, a dark shadow appeared.
    - A dark shadow appeared as soon as they closed the door.
    - They closed the door. A dark shadow appeared.
- Explore grammatical concepts and terms in the context of text purpose, helping pupils to see what effect can be achieved on the audience, for example:
    - Use of modal verbs and adverbs of possibility to persuade an audience: *we could possibly ban mobile phones in school/we should probably ban mobile phones in school/we must definitely ban mobile phones in school.*
    - Use of the passive voice with the agent removed to help a technical write-up sound more official: *Every minute, Sam measured the temperature of the water.* Compare with: *Every minute, the temperature of the water was measured.*

HANDWRITING

The pen is the tongue of the mind.

Horace, a Roman poet

HANDWRITTEN

The subject of handwriting raises impassioned opinions in education. Is there a place for it in modern society? Is there a place for it in primary schools? The DfE seems to think so; handwriting objectives are firmly embedded within the end-of-key-stage expectations. The end goal is for all children to master a fluent, cursive script.

Fifty years ago, this would not have been a controversial aim. While telephones and telegrams had lessened the need for letter writing, compulsory education from ages 5 to 16 in the UK drove the literacy agenda. Children learned to write so that they might learn via writing. And that meant handwriting. Computers were in their infancy, and typewriters, though prevalent, were generally a work tool to be mastered if required rather than an integrated means of communication. But as technology progressed, some schools were failing to 'see the writing on the wall'.

In the last couple of years, we have all witnessed the revolution in artificial intelligence (AI). Considering the awesome feats it has already achieved, will there really be a need for the next generation to acquire any writing skills at all? It's a sobering thought. However, crystal-ball gazing to determine what skills may no longer be needed in the future isn't a reason to abandon something immediately. And beyond the obvious capabilities of current and future technology, there is surely another side to handwriting beyond the functional skill.

HANDCRAFTED

Handwriting is part of you: your personality, your soul. It builds a deep connection to your reader in a way that a keyboard can't.

Natalie Goldberg has written dozens of books on the art and craft of writing. In *Writing Down the Bones* (2005), she says that when she needs to write something emotional, she must write it first time by hand on paper because she feels that her handwriting – or indeed anyone's handwriting – 'is more connected to the movement of the heart'.

Many would agree that we imprint a little of ourselves onto the world when we put pen to paper. When we teach our youngest pupils to mark-make and they begin their journey of encoding the spoken word, we equip them with the skills to make an emotional connection with their world as much as a literary one. Parents and carers often proudly retain their children's early attempts at writing. It's not surprising that a handwritten card with misspelled words and malformed letters is treasured long after a perfectly produced greeting from an online company has been sent to recycling.

Handwriting has long been seen as something that can reveal much about a person's character or emotional state. Teachers are more attuned than many, perhaps, to 'graphology' – the science of handwriting. Just as phones are equipped with facial recognition, primary school teachers swiftly learn the skill of recognising the authors of unnamed pieces of homework, abandoned worksheets or unclaimed notes. Almost as quickly as new names are learned at the beginning of the school year, so teachers learn to match pupils with their unique stamp on the world: their handwriting.

As humans, we do seem predisposed to leave that graphical imprint; our marking is almost an extension of our fingerprint. From early cave paintings, through Roman graffiti, to Samuel Pepys' diaries, Victorian photographs or even the calling card of the inimitable Banksy, we want to say, 'We were here'. The root word *graph* comes from the Ancient Greek language, where it means 'written down, printed or drawn'. Just like any form of graphics, we can bring our own style and personality to, or even just get a sense of artistic pride from our own calligraphy.

So, if nothing else, handwriting tuition should be maintained as it gives pupils an important form of artistic communication.

While it may be a step too far to suggest that teachers can determine pupils' personality traits through their calligraphy, it is true that teachers will often be able to make some judgements about a pupil as they read through a handwritten piece of text. The script might reveal something about the pupil's level of engagement with the task, their mood or even how quickly they were working.

In society, assumptions are often made about a person's level of attainment – or even perhaps their level of intelligence – by looking at their handwriting. Perhaps this is a relic of a time when not everyone had received literary instruction. Mahatma Gandhi (1929) was said to be ashamed of his own handwriting as it revealed that he had not had the same level of education as others: 'I tried later to improve mine, but it was too late. I could never repair the neglect of my youth. Let every young man and woman be warned by my example, and understand that good handwriting is a necessary part of education.'

While times – and educators – have moved on, a high value is still placed on 'beautiful' handwriting. Likewise, there is an expectation that, along with spelling and grammar, a fluent, joined, legible script is an indicator of age-related attainment. Exceptions can be made for specific pupils in specific cases, but for everyone else there is a standard to be met.

TEACHING HANDWRITING

If we accept that handwriting is, for the time being at least, an important part of primary education, how best should we approach its instruction?

The act of writing is a complex, fine-motor skill. Before children can be expected to write, they need to develop gross-motor skills that will support the hand and arm movements, and build core strength and flexibility. The development of such skills can be supported by arm-strengthening activities like skipping, as well as movements designed to 'cross the mid-line' diagonally and from left to right, such as clapping games and ribbon twirling. Dexterity is key and this can be developed through fine-motor-skill activities such as threading cotton reels and tracing shapes with fingers in sand.

Once pupils are ready to mark-make, start them off with large tools such as chunky crayons and big paintbrushes. Another precursor to handwriting is the drawing of patterns that mimic the strokes and directions of letters. These lead naturally into independently made marks that begin to resemble numbers and letters. Pupils can continue to practise letter shapes in activities such as 'drawing' the letter shapes in the air with a wand, on their friend's back with their finger, or on the playground with a paintbrush dipped in water.

One of my own pet hates is incorrect pencil grip. I have seen too many children (and adults) struggling with a hooked or fist grip, or a pencil precariously balanced between too few fingers. For most children, an awkward grip will result in poor letter formation as well as causing discomfort and muscle fatigue that will impact writing stamina. Like many bad habits, poor pencil grip is incredibly difficult to undo once established. It is, therefore, imperative that a more natural, traditional grip is taught and encouraged from the outset.

Equally, body position and paper slant are factors that are often overlooked when supporting children's handwriting. They need to be addressed from the start to promote writing comfort and ease.

Handwriting instruction should teach groups of letters in the same 'families' – in other words, those that have similar formation – such as tall letters, letters containing oblique strokes or those that 'start like a c'. Ensure everyone uses the same agreed terminology and uses the same spoken mnemonics to support letter formation (such as, 'start at the top, all the way down and over the bridge'). Consistency of details like these is key, especially for pupils who are struggling in this area.

JOINING

The Reading Framework (DfE, 2023a) urges schools to consider delaying the teaching of joined handwriting while the muscles in children's shoulders, arms and hands are still developing. Pupils in Reception still struggle with the manual dexterity needed to control writing implements.

Once a school has decided when pupils should start joining, staff need to decide on a uniform approach. School policy should be clear upon the expectations around how to teach joined handwriting, including consistency around which letters join and which are best left unjoined.

Above all, every teacher in the school must model that handwriting approach in everything they do. It has to be a 'do as I do, not do as I say' approach for there to be impact. It's surprising how often I see vast discrepancies from class to class within the same school.

PRACTICE MAKES PERFECT

Automaticity in transcription skills is vital in terms of lessening the cognitive load on the brain and freeing up capacity for other writing skills including ideation. If pupils are to develop an accurate, legible, fluent script, it stands to reason that handwriting must be discretely taught, actively modelled and routinely practised. If handwriting is poor across the school, or within a cohort, more time needs to be dedicated to this skill than in places where a high standard in handwriting is already established. Similarly, individual pupils might need extra support and time to practise this skill. Even once the basic letter formation has been secured, consistency might be an issue.

PUBLISHING

One of the most motivating things a school can do to improve handwriting standards has nothing to do with choice of schemes, media or extrinsic rewards.

When a school places a high value on handwriting – and *demonstrates* that – pupils will pay more attention to their presentation and handwriting. If teachers and classroom assistants model the school's preferred script on the board, when they give feedback in books or even when they write to each other, pupils will generally aspire to emulate it.

We all have that particular handwriting that we reserve for special occasions; maybe writing a birthday card or leaving a message in a guest book. For teachers, it's also the handwriting that the pupils will see leading the way. This is the handwriting for public consumption; for publishing. It needs to be top notch. For pupils, this might be the writing of theirs that goes on display on a wall or in a book. This is when you really want pupils to roll out the red carpet and bring out their gold standard. If handwriting skills have been taught sequentially and rigorously, we ensure they can.

ASIDE

Other than which scheme to buy, which implements to use and the relative merits or evils of the pen licence, one aspect of handwriting seems to be the most divisive in primary schools:

To lead in or not to lead in? That is the question.

Lead-ins in handwriting can enhance legibility and consistency. They aim to provide a clear starting point for each letter, reducing confusion around formation and direction. This is especially beneficial when writing in cursive. Lead-ins can also help maintain a consistent slant and spacing, resulting in a more polished and professional look.

However, while in-strokes can improve legibility, they can also be problematic for pupils at the beginning of their handwriting journey. In its 2023 report, 'Validation of systematic synthetic phonics programmes: supporting documentation', the DfE attests that the extra strokes needed to form letters with lead-ins cause 'unnecessary difficulty for beginners' (DfE, 2023b). Authorities on handwriting, including the National Handwriting Association (Hulme, n.d.), concur.

Ultimately, the decision of whether to use lead-ins depends on schools' personal preference. Since 2021, however, the new advice for teaching phonics has influenced schools in terms of choosing a handwriting scheme. The guidance for providers of SSP schemes is that all resources designed for pupils should be in print. It stands to reason that lead-ins will put extra visual demands on an inexperienced reader.

Because continuity and consistency are essential when teaching handwriting, few would advocate starting in print and moving to joined handwriting with lead-in strokes; the letters are formed differently in each case. But letter formation is practised alongside letter recognition. Because schools adopting a scheme with entry strokes will need to teach it from the outset to avoid disruption, they are left with a dilemma.

INDEPENDENCE

The greatest sign of success for a teacher ... is to be able to say, 'The children are now working as if I did not exist'.

Maria Montessori

Let's take a moment to consider what complex writing processes might feel like for the learner and how we might support pupils with skills gaps.

As with any learning, pupils move through the stages made familiar to all teachers by Vygotsky (1978). From 'what I cannot do at all, even with help' through to 'what I can do independently' via the zone of proximal development (or 'what I can do with assistance'). With writing, the zone of proximal development is broad and deep. Which aspect of the writing process needs support for any given pupil at any given time? It could be letter formation, spelling, generating ideas or all of these. Some pupils may just need a guiding hand to pull it all together in a timely or coherent fashion.

Assisted learning should take many forms. While most would agree that pupils who can't work independently should not automatically or permanently work with an adult, the reality is that many pupils who struggle become reliant on support. In fact, they often appear to be glued to a classroom assistant. The best intentions can unwittingly create a learned helplessness from which it may be difficult to wean a child. Some pupils become so reliant on an adult that little is achieved when no one is available, and some flatly refuse to work unaided.

If you have pupils who lack any independence and appear to 'Velcro' themselves to adults, aim to build their stamina in terms of how long they will work unaided.

During a session with a pupil, move back and forth between varying levels of support ('I do, we do, you do'). Switch between modelling and demonstrating ('I do'), joint writing to prompt and guide while the pupil has a go ('we do'), to times where the pupil works largely unsupported ('you do'). Insist that you move away at times while the pupil writes independently. Gradually increase the 'you do' time, but try to come back to 'we do' to reassure and praise.

The trick is to build in metacognition and self-help strategies along the route to independence so the pupil has alternative routes to success other than to ask for help.

In five 30-minute sessions over a week, this could look something like this:

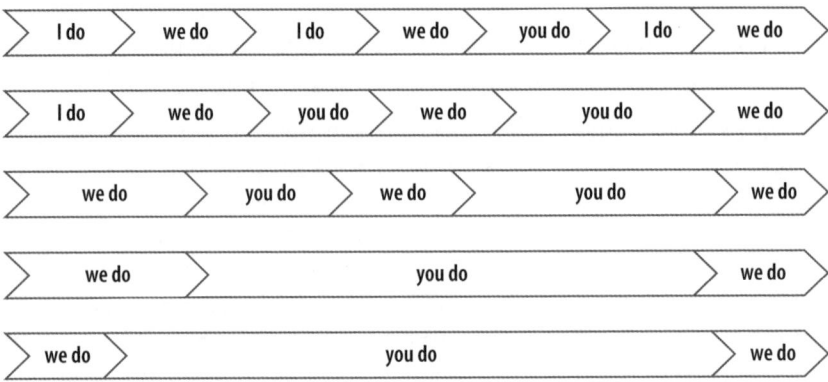

As we become independently competent at a new skill, whether it be taking our first hesitant baby steps, acquiring an additional language or mastering a musical instrument, we move through a further continuum of learning (as described by Fitts and Posner's three-stage model, 1967).

Imagine yourself with a newly acquired skill such as driving. The first step is the cognitive stage, where you are having to think consciously about the processes (such as how to change gear or checking mirrors). You might seek external feedback in order to improve.

Time and deliberate practice will lead you to the next step, known as the associative stage, where you make fewer mistakes and have more consistency. Here you begin to connect the dots as you build your schema. You will be able to problem-solve and fix your own mistakes. Again, the old adage 'practice makes perfect' is key here.

Finally, you move through to the autonomous stage, at which point you are performing a task accurately, without any effort. In this example, learning to drive has become a subconscious skill where you are not constantly chanting 'mirror, signal, manoeuvre' under your breath.

While this continuum tends to be associated purely with physical skills, one might argue that the concepts are equally applicable to development in writing (and after all, writing employs motor skills too). As adults, it is likely we are in the autonomous stage for writing: we don't have to think consciously about whether to add in a capital letter after a full stop, how to spell the words we want to use or even whether a letter 'p' should stand on the line or go under it. At this stage, cognitive load is not consumed with the mechanics of a skill; these skills are deployed fluently and automatically now.

At the autonomous stage, the brain is freed up for a learner to master the skill; to enhance and craft it to become more effective at it. Furthermore, the skill becomes transferable to different situations. Just as an autonomous driver might be unfazed by driving a hire car in the dark, abroad, with children crying on the back seat, autonomous writers can use their writerly skills and knowledge seamlessly across a variety of writing tasks.

SCAFFOLDING

But many pupils won't be quite there yet. While they can theoretically work unaided, the conscious effort required may take its toll on writing stamina, and for some pupils, falling 'off task' is easy at this stage. The need for reassurance is great. Getting pupils off to a confident start with the task is key. As Maria Montessori (1967) once said:

> The child's development follows a path of successive stages of independence, and our knowledge of this must guide us in our behaviour towards him.

Consider pre-teaching concepts, skills or vocabulary and pre-reading a text so that when a pupil revisits the learning in the lesson, it feels more familiar. Provide explicit instructions, perhaps recording steps to learning so the pupil can play it back for reference, or even as dual-coded directives including images. Build in time for joint planning of writing tasks, including oral rehearsal.

Inability to work independently can be exacerbated in the race through the school year to 'cover' all the age-related objectives for English. For pupils who have found the previous task difficult, it may feel as though teachers are constantly moving the goalposts to make the task harder and harder. Is there ever an opportunity for the pupil to practise a previously supported activity unaided to build confidence and independence rather than constantly struggling to master new learning?

If the writing always seems too tricky to be completed unaided, try to build in times where the task is deliberately set to generate success and completion. Learning happens in that 'Goldilocks zone': if it is too easy, there is no new learning; however, a task that is too difficult will lead only to frustration. But the easier end of that zone allows for a different kind of learning: discovering resilience, independence and what success feel like.

Try keeping the same success criteria for a few days. Mark each objective with an 'i' for 'independently' or 's' for 'supported' and expect the proportion of independent criteria to increase over each lesson (see the following figure). This way, it is easy for the pupil and teacher to spot those little steps of progress that might otherwise be missed.

Success Criteria
- I can draw the pictures in order using the actions to help me remember the sequence. (S) prompts
- I can use arrows to link the story together. (I)
- I can add key words and phrases to help me retell the story. (S) prompts

Marking success criteria with an 'i' or an 's' can help teachers to monitor progress.

INDEPENDENCE

Reliance on adults tends to be born out of a lack of confidence. Pupils may not be clear as to why they are not experiencing the success in writing that others enjoy, but they will be aware that they find it tough. Peer co-construction is a great halfway house between adult support and independent writing.

One way of doing this is for pairs of pupils to discuss what they are going to write and for both pupils to record the same sentence, supporting each other with transcriptional elements as they do so. When they are both ready, they move on to the next sentence.

Alternatively, pairs of pupils can take it in turn to write sentences that they have both orally rehearsed. In the example shown in the following figure the pupil writing the second sentence always found an excuse to avoid writing. But when paired with another child she was motivated to add her own sentence and even correct some of her partner's!

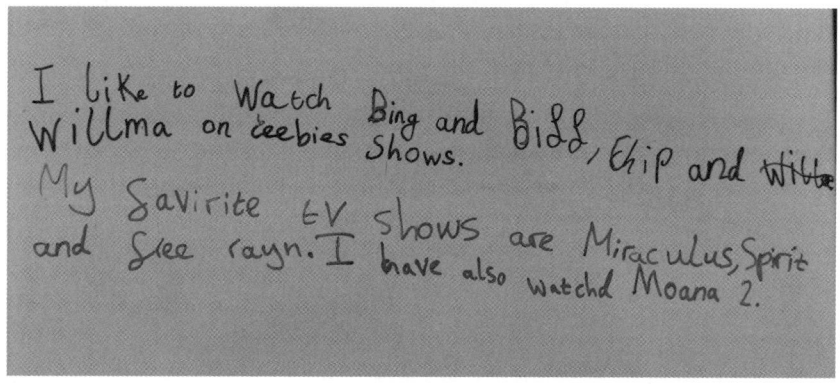

When pupils work in pairs, it can benefit the less confident learner.

There are myriad ways of scaffolding learning in English beyond providing adult support. It may be that pupils *do* feel confident in some aspects of their writing but not in others. In the same way that adults scaffolding the task provides access to learning, physical prompts can give pupils the 'leg-up' they need to meet the objectives of a lesson that they are less confident about. From phoneme frames to word banks, annotated models to sentence checklists, pupils will benefit from resources that they can use to prompt, cross-reference or simply reassure.

Pupils need to be taught how and when prompts can be used so that they can employ them effectively. They should be freely available on tables so that pupils don't feel self-conscious about picking them up. These sorts of prompts are useful to all pupils in a class but make a vital difference to some children, lessening cognitive load while building independence.

Use of technology can do wonders for building independence and allowing pupils to focus on specific parts of the writing process. Speech-to-text apps temporarily free pupils from the transcriptional elements of writing and allow them to focus on composition and publishing. Software programs can provide visual and auditory prompts to help with sentence structure and text organisation.

The key to all scaffolding – whether it be stabilisers on a bike, adults on hand or line guides – is that it is a temporary aid. In learning terms, a plan should always be in place to withdraw the support gradually and take the learner to the final independent stage. If there are pupils in class who need the same sorts of scaffolding for every lesson, it's worth examining the tasks to review that plan.

When pupils are being assessed, we need to consider the extent to which the task was performed unaided, and it is vital to make clear distinctions. A pupil is not reading at an age-related level if they can only answer questions on appropriately pitched texts that are read to them. Similarly, a writing task is not independent if it is barely distinguishable from the written model shared by the teacher.

However, it is possible to consider the individual elements of a writing task when making judgements. For example, a pupil may have worked on a task unaided but received help to correct spelling mistakes. Nonetheless, we can assess their ability to structure a text, weave in the grammatical elements or use appropriate vocabulary. We might even be able to see how far they can apply certain spelling skills. What we can't do is say that they are able to independently edit their own writing … yet.

Finally, the route to independence is through carefully sequencing and spacing skills so that new knowledge builds on prior learning. Pupils need to draw upon what they know in order to self-scaffold into new skills. Where the foundational learning is embedded and the rungs on the ladder are carefully spaced, most pupils will learn to climb with just a little prompting. When the ladder is not secured at the base and there are missing rungs, they will need ropes, support and a lot of encouragement to make the ascent.

ASIDE

Building independence gradually is key, especially for pupils who are reliant on specific support and cannot yet evaluate that aspect of their work unaided. For example, we cannot suddenly stop pointing out spelling errors without giving them the skills to self-regulate their own spelling. This might include teaching them strategies for remembering certain spelling rules, providing tools such as phoneme frames and charts to help build words, and modelling how to use them.

Proofreading strategies could be shared, starting with monitoring on a sentence-by-sentence basis and building up to larger amounts of text. Older pupils might need support to navigate a dictionary.

At this point, you are ready to move away from giving or correcting spellings to a pupil independently monitoring their own writing for errors. Try the following staggered approach to independence:

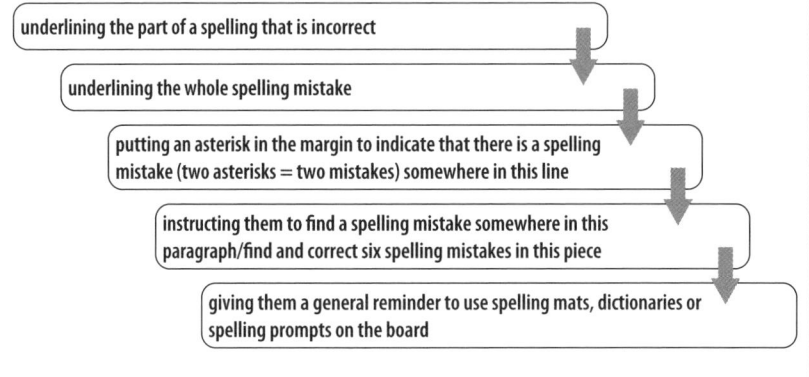

JOURNEY

Curriculum is a narrative; it's about building layers of knowledge and understanding in a coherent sequence that helps children make connections and see the bigger picture.

Mary Myatt

If you are a 'glass-half-full' type of person, you'll recall that each year almost 75% of Year 6 pupils entered for reading SATs achieve the expected standard. The figure is slightly lower in writing attainment, but still provides cause to celebrate. But the pessimist in me sees the flip side and notes that just under 3 children in 10 leave the primary phase ill-equipped to face the reading and writing demands of the KS3 curriculum.

As mentioned before, when we dig deeper into these figures, we see that there is a persistently stubborn gap between children facing economic disadvantage and their non-disadvantaged peers.

Not always – but often – it is the learners from economically disadvantaged backgrounds who have gaps in their knowledge. These gaps, combined with a disjointed, illogical curricular approach, make it harder for such pupils to build schemata on which to map and connect their learning. Gaps in understanding and missed learning lead to holes in that knowledge web, weaker connections and, ultimately, more gaps.

SEQUENCING THE ENGLISH CURRICULUM

A poorly sequenced curriculum exacerbates this issue as it fails to build skills in a logical, systematic fashion and doesn't provide opportunities to revisit and build upon prior learning. Pupils with a strong and established schema for learning are confident enough to ride out the odd incongruity and may even be able to draw on existing knowledge to make sense of it.

In writing, for example, they could tolerate the occasional randomly taught spelling rule or grammatical concept. Those with gaps, however, will struggle to make any connections and may, therefore, fail to assimilate this new learning. An existing lack of confidence may potentially lead to self-blame and disconnect: 'This doesn't make sense, but it is probably my fault.'

As Dan Nicholls (2022a) attests, 'It is the year-on-year progression through a cumulatively sufficient curriculum that is the biggest opportunity and the best bet for disadvantaged learners to close the gap.'

THE WRITING CHALLENGE

Of each of the English curriculum areas, writing has bounced back the least well since the disruption of the Covid-19 pandemic. The sticking points are largely the same for all pupils: a struggle with the skills of punctuation and sentence structure; handwriting and spelling lacking security and automaticity; and limited vocabulary impacting on composition.

Pulling together the various skills involved in writing is a huge challenge. Add gaps in learning and understanding into the mix and it is no wonder that children can feel utterly overwhelmed when asked to write.

SECURING FOUNDATIONAL SKILLS

The most recent version of the national curriculum (DfE, 2013b) does sequence learning across the primary phase. But pupils do not necessarily learn in a neat, linear form, and there can be a difference between what is taught and what is caught. When mapping out pupils' writing journey, it is vital to look beyond the confines of their year group expectations and plot in opportunities to revisit learning from earlier in the writing journey.

Education adviser Mary Myatt (2022) suggests, 'One of the most efficient ways to sequence the curriculum is to identify the concepts or big ideas in the content we are teaching.' Knowing 'what constitutes a sentence' is perhaps the biggest idea in the teaching and learning of primary writing. Without it, nothing else hangs right.

And yet, you may be seeing more pupils than ever before entering KS2 with a weak knowledge of sentence structure, largely demonstrated by their inaccurate use of punctuation. This issue is a significant barrier to progress as the expectations around manipulation of clauses, punctuation and general cohesion of writing get ever more demanding as pupils move through the curriculum. It is, therefore, crucial that weaknesses in sentence structure are addressed before moving on.

The national curriculum has high expectations for grammar, but these expectations are deliberately stripped back at KS1 and build gradually. While there is a huge emphasis on application of phonics knowledge for encoding, punctuation is limited to securing the concept of a sentence: using capital letters to start; full stops, question marks and exclamation marks to end. Adjectives, conjunctions (other than *and*), adverbs and speech punctuation all come later.

As well as providing clarity around the sequence and progression of learning, this stripped-back approach allows time for the deep knowledge of what a sentence looks, sounds and feels like to be embedded.

It can be tempting to race through the curriculum, either to recover what is perceived to be lost ground, or even because a concept is judged to have been sufficiently taught. However, we support pupils more by going back to basics rather than pushing them to 'run before they can walk'. It may feel anxiety inducing when we look at the end-of-year/end-of-phase expectations, but securing those foundational skills is the key to pupils making stronger, faster progress.

And no matter how counter-intuitive it may feel, we generally need to go back further than we might imagine. To use a gardening metaphor, we need to prune right back to the last strong piece of growth and build from there. If we trim back too lightly, we achieve little new growth; but if we are brave and go far enough, pupils' learning will flourish and come back more vigorously.

It is vital that writing models demonstrate sentence structures that the pupils can and should emulate in their own writing. It's easy to get carried away when modelling for pupils; to present examples that go far beyond the sentence structures we can expect them to be able to construct independently. This can lead pupils to try to learn by rote or become over-reliant on the model. Take the following sentence as an example:

Once upon a time, there lived a girl who was called Little Red Riding Hood, because of the long, red cloak she always wore.

While this is a lovely example of storytelling language that children might hear, read and enjoy in Year 1, further analysis reveals: a prepositional phrase, a relative clause, use of the passive voice, a subordinating conjunction, adjectives, adverbs and a comma to boot. The challenge is to synthesise a reading model into a pitch-appropriate writing model that matches the sequencing of skills and provides stepping stones to independence along the way.

SPELLING FOUNDATIONS

The national curriculum's spelling programme of study is robustly designed. It is clearly sequenced, with objectives building over the years in a logical, systematic way. The continuing role of phonics for encoding is made clear: 'Phonic knowledge should continue to underpin spelling after Key Stage 1; teachers should still draw pupils' attention to GPCs that do and do not fit in with what has been taught so far' (DfE, 2013a). However, while the curriculum does explicitly state that each year group should revisit previous rules and concepts, it doesn't shout loudly enough about this requirement.

As a result, many schemes dive straight into new teaching for each year group with merely a cursory nod – or no nod at all – towards prior learning. A strong spelling scheme is one that purposefully and systematically reviews previous learning. It is not learning from the week before or the lesson before, but linked learning that forms the foundation for progress. It recognises that high-value spellings are introduced early in the curriculum because they will be used with a higher frequency.

It therefore makes sense to re-teach these areas term after term, year after year. This is not about interventions for pupils who have fallen behind. This is about making orthographical connections; reigniting and reinforcing prior learning in order to go deeper, add complexity and help secure new concepts.

READING CONNECTIONS

Reading is simultaneously simple to sequence and the hardest of the disciplines.

At the earliest phase of reading, it is straightforward enough to gradually introduce skills and behaviours that are precursors to reading (such as distinguishing sounds in the environment, finding the rhythm of body percussion, orally segmenting or blending words). Experts have set out the order in which graphemes for reading should be met. Gradually, through a systematic, synthetic phonics programme, pupils acquire the GPCs that enable decoding. By the end of their Reception year, pupils should know one graphemic correspondence for each of the 44 phonemes in the English language. One way of reading each grapheme, one way of recording each sound.

During the review part of the lesson, pupils recall previously learned letters or words. By Year 1, the revisiting of linked prior learning is fast and furious: pupils are introduced to new GPCs, new ways of reading existing graphemes and new spellings for existing phonemes. The connections need to be made and so we circle back.

We must acknowledge that the phonics screening check is a low bar: recognising between 32 and 40 words in isolation does not a secure reader make. It is possible to 'pass' the phonics screening check using knowledge of GPCs almost entirely taught in Reception. And, of course, the check is purely about decoding decontextualised single words; there is no application of these words in context for stamina or comprehension.

Aside from phonics for decoding, the progression and sequencing for reading is about the pitch of a text. If we remove the level of difficulty provided by the decodability of words, the measure of pitch will include various other quantifiable aspects such as:

- comprehensibility of vocabulary (generally determined by a word's frequency in common lexicon)

- number of words per sentence, giving us the complexity of sentence structure
- number of words in the entire text, which will determine the stamina needed to get through the book.

These elements can be numericised into a 'lexile' value for the book – a value that is used by some digital reading programmes as well as standardised tests. Of course, more difficult to quantify is the subject matter, which will also determine the pitch of a text.

In essence, the elements that we can use to assess pupils for comprehension remain the same or largely similar throughout our reading journey. What changes is the level of difficulty of a text. However, in the same way that we could choose to use simpler sentence structures or more basic vocabulary in our writing, reading shouldn't always be about spiralling upwards.

Just because you *can* read Shakespeare and Swift doesn't mean you always *want* to do so. In fact, when reading for pleasure, you might be more likely to choose anyone but those authors, even if you admire their work. But aside from the joy that can be found by a Year 6 pupil in picking up a picture book or whizzing through a book with a much lower reading age than they have attained, there are practical reasons for sometimes choosing an easier book.

When we introduce a new reading skill for pupils (such as learning to infer meaning) or when we are trying to impart more substantive knowledge in another subject area, it is useful to be able to use a lower-pitched text. This means that the pupils can focus on the new skill or take in the new information rather than desperately trying to decode the text at the same time.

Similarly, we might want the pupils to build reading stamina by taking on longer books. For some children, a drop in pitch might afford them the resilience to read more.

Lastly, when trying to build fluency and confidence in young readers, we might drop back a step to enable pupils to read independently today what they read with the support of an adult yesterday.

With built-in opportunities to revisit skills and knowledge, a school bakes in security around confidence in English. As well as mopping up any missed learning, revisiting knowledge gives pupils another chance to consolidate concepts before taking on new, related learning. It's about strengthening connections and ensuring foundations are solid before adding layers. A strong curriculum is a spiral curriculum, circling back and scooping up as it reaches forward.

ASIDE

Take a look at each aspect of language provision in your curriculum: phonics, comprehension, spelling, handwriting, grammar and even oracy. Ask yourself the following:

- Can you see a clear progression of skills mapped out?
- Is that progression systematic, logical and cumulative?
- Is the pace appropriate or does it race on without securing foundational skills?
- What are the opportunities for revisiting and reinforcing prior learning in each year group?
- What provision is made for pupils who arrive in school without some of those early skills in place or for those who struggle to retain learning?

KNOWING

The key features of effective learning environments are that they create student engagement and allow teachers, learners, and their peers to ensure that the learning is proceeding in the intended direction. The only way we can do this is through assessment. That is why assessment is, indeed, the bridge between teaching and learning.

Dylan Wiliam

When the concept of a 'national curriculum' was introduced to the UK in 1988, it brought with it the possibility of standardised assessment for primary-aged children. The original raft of tests for the ends of KS1 and KS2 have been stripped back over the years (much to the relief of most practitioners), but for better or worse, schools are now in the habit of measuring, assessing and judging children from the time they arrive in primary school to the time they leave.

One of the aspects of teaching English that seems so tricky to get right is that of assessment. Granted, some areas of the subject can be subjected to a quantifiable analysis. A spelling is either right or wrong, and a pupil either read a word correctly or they didn't. But many more areas are trickier to substantiate, such as what constitutes 'good story writing' or an 'age-related sentence'. Without a binary measure, it can also be very challenging to be truly objective when it comes to assessing pupils in our charge. We bring to bear background knowledge of the pupil – or even the nature of the task – that can be difficult to disconnect from the judgement.

Changes to the system over the years have arguably removed one layer of stress and replaced it with another.

The cessation of externally marked writing at Year 6 led to the introduction of teacher assessments and external moderators instead. The departure of levels and sub-levels made way for a system of secure-fit statements that can feel open to interpretation and lead to confusion. There is plenty of support for understanding the level descriptors for the end of Year 6, so teachers new to the year group need to be given time to familiarise themselves with the guidance and exemplification materials.

Knowing the parameters within which judgements are to be made is crucial to getting accurate and standardised data.

MEASURING AND WEIGHING

Tests like the Year 1 phonics screening check, the Year 6 reading SAT and the grammar, punctuation and spelling (GPS) paper provide just a snapshot in time. They offer a numerical value to show what pupils have managed to retain and demonstrate in one short appraisal. Summative judgements at the end of the year, therefore, have limited value to the current class teacher. It is vital that staff members across the school cooperate to focus on a pupil's complete learning journey rather than the destination. Information gleaned from summative assessments needs to be triangulated with ongoing formative assessment to identify any gaps in learning and highlight next steps.

When the subject of assessment is raised, conversation can develop a porcine theme. We acknowledge that overuse of summative assessment is akin to constantly 'weighing pigs': frequently repeating tests doesn't improve pupils' subject knowledge and won't necessarily yield improved scores. Instead, time is better spent 'fattening pigs' by stuffing them with knowledge and building the appropriate skills and confidence. However, the key to fattening pigs well is to get the diet completely right.

To best support all pupils in their charge, teachers need an absolute knowledge of the English curriculum from Early Years to Year 6, combined with an in-depth knowledge of all pupils.

In short, they need to know the current attainment of individual pupils at any given time for any piece of learning. Not the holistic knowledge of whether their reading or writing is at the age-related standard, but granular-level knowledge of which skill is holding them back: detailed knowledge such as specific letter formation in handwriting, spelling of Year 2 common exception words or punctuation of dialogue. What related knowledge is secure and what does the pupil need to do to fix the next piece of learning in place?

To make that knowledge stick, a pupil's strengths and interests need to be brought into the mix. Consider how each child learns best and shape their learning to harness the positive and break the barriers. Do this constantly to plug each gap. This is assessment for learning at its best.

PHONICS ACQUISITION

An SSP scheme will provide materials for the regular assessment of pupils. However, in general these are based on single-grapheme or word-level checks. For these tests to be anything more than summative, they need to be analysed carefully to determine the pupil's next steps. Not how many words a pupil got wrong, but the nature of each mistake. A pupil may have struggled with the number of graphemes in a word, been unable to blend the word or experienced difficulties with specific GPCs.

Like the phonics screening check, these 'box' tests give you just one part of the picture: how well pupils can recognise letters or words on a given day. They will provide information about who might need more support and in which areas, but if such tests follow what has been taught in order to discover what has been caught, the learning gaps have already begun to appear. For a more holistic and immediate picture, regular formative assessments need to be woven into teaching, including observation of pupils' learning covering:

- phonics lessons/teaching sequences
- adult-led activities including guided reading/shared reading
- child initiated learning/independent non-core subjects
- application during independent writing.

Analysis should also take account of pupils' ability to read individual words in the context of reading a complete text (running records, diagnostic miscue analysis).

Ideally, aim for 80% assessment of embedded skills, 20% discrete word reading tests.

Constant scanning and responsive teaching support a deep knowledge of what each pupil can clearly or nearly do, as well as determine where support to keep up needs to be directed. It's the difference between assessment and assumption.

READING

In a test of reading comprehension, you will undoubtedly collect information about how successfully pupils were able to answer a series of questions and analyse the types of questions they got wrong. If the pupils are confident readers and are experienced at analysing and discussing texts, you'll be looking at the sorts of comprehension questions that might need more of a focus and concentrate on this area. But looking through the scripts won't offer much information on reading behaviours and barriers to success. This knowledge is especially key for pupils with low scores across the board or for young children who are beginning their reading journey.

The key to accurate reading assessment is to listen to children read individually. How do they approach the text? What does their body language tell you? Observe how well they maintain accuracy, speed and expression as they go along and how quickly they lose stamina.

In terms of comprehension, consider the following as pupils read aloud:

- How does the pupil tackle questions you ask them? Perhaps they:
    - start at the beginning and re-read the whole text until they find the answer
    - skim the text looking for key words
    - try to remember what they have read or just take a wild stab based on their background knowledge.

- Analyse the skills a pupil is using when they meet a word they don't understand. Do they:
  - wait for an adult to prompt them
  - try to use context, perhaps by trying to substitute a word that would make sense
  - look for clues within the word
  - consider a link with a word that they do know?

Once you have a clearer picture of the strengths and weaknesses of a pupil's read-aloud skills, you can address these during further reading instruction. Support the pupil to understand the specific areas of focus and teach self-monitoring skills. Use prompts to encourage re-reading. Guide and scaffold their reading sessions with this knowledge in mind.

CHECK FOR STUDENT UNDERSTANDING: SPELLING

There's a lot of 'knowing' needed in education, and spelling is no exception. There are over 100 separate spelling objectives for pupils to master between Year 1 and Year 6, and dozens of words that exemplify each one. This necessitates teacher subject knowledge of the entire spelling journey as well as an understanding of how to impart that knowledge efficiently and effectively.

Even assuming that the transference of knowledge has been successful, we cannot necessarily be sure that the knowledge will stick. Continuously evaluating pupils' spelling application during independent writing facilitates immediate feedback and informs upcoming discrete sessions. Having ascertained the starting pitch, monitor individual performance at each stage of the teaching sequence and adapt teaching to meet all learners' needs.

The review part of a spelling sequence will be invaluable for reigniting past learning, firing up connections and assessing pupils' understanding before they build the next layer of learning. Establish what prior knowledge might be useful to today's learning. Spelling accurately relies on ensuring that each piece of the puzzle fits together and thereby requires mechanisms for regular checking along the way.

The true testament of understanding is whether the pupil can explain what they now know about when to use this spelling pattern. At this point, any misconceptions can be swiftly addressed and you can decide about where to take the learning next.

Weekly and/or monthly testing is something that we often see associated with spelling instruction. Again, there are easy tweaks that can be made to increase not only the enjoyment of spelling assessment, but also the efficacy of it:

- Dictations are helpful in supporting pupils to see the words they have been exploring in context, rather than in isolation. Dropping previously taught words, perhaps common exception words, into dictations over time will support their retention.
- Asking pupils, in pairs, to look through their independent writing for errors, test each other back and forth and support each other with corrections can be very helpful to identify and fix common errors.
- Pre-testing a spelling rule or convention with a list of words at the start of a sequence will not only provide valuable assessment for learning, but will also allow a post-sequence test to give a clear indication of progress for each individual pupil. You could score the difference between their pre- and post-test, rather than their score out of 10.

BUILDING A CLEAR PICTURE OF SKILLS ACROSS A DISCIPLINE: WRITING

When carrying out writing judgements, ensure that you are building a picture across several pieces of work at a time. Remember that, across a collection of writing, there will be some pieces that are stronger than others, and that within each piece, there will be elements that are more or less secure. Consider each skill in isolation and look at how consistently the pupil is applying it. Use the Never, Occasionally, Frequently, Always or Naturally (NOFAN) approach to assess whether they demonstrate this skill.

This is especially handy to do with punctuation. How reliable is the pupil's use of full stops and capital letters, for example? Beyond Year 1, those skills are an absolute non-negotiable and we need to see them consistently employed across all writing. If this skill is not secure, intervene and consolidate that learning, using constant monitoring to focus teaching and learning until the pupil moves along that NOFAN scale. As and when additional punctuation is taught, each skill might expect to move from 'never' to 'natural' in the same way. Isolation enables judgements to be formed for each skill and teaching can be adapted accordingly.

If a pupil can confidently and fluently read texts at the pitch and in the quantity expected at the end of the year, any test they need to do will be relatively easy to prepare for. Likewise, pupils taught to analyse language in the books they read and use grammar and punctuation in context of their own writing will be able to identify these elements when tested. To achieve that, we need to have high expectations of all learners. We can help all pupils to succeed if we understand what is needed to make that happen.

ASIDE

From an early age, most pupils become very aware of what they can do with ease, and where they struggle. Develop this understanding and harness it to triangulate your knowledge of them. Where pupils lack that self-awareness, support them to gain a better understanding of their learning strengths and barriers to learning, as well as what and who helps them.

Where possible, carry out conferencing alongside pupils and their writing:

- Encourage them to point out things they are proud of, aspects of the learning that they found difficult and what they would like assistance with.
- Assess how well they articulate their understanding and address any misconceptions.
- Decide whether any errors were simply overlooked or whether there was a gap in knowledge.

- Evaluate together whether overall outcomes, such as incomplete tasks or untidy handwriting, are down to time constraints or the pupil's emotional state at the time.
- Tell them what you think they need to work on next, keeping steps small and manageable.
- Together, consider what needs to be done and how it will be achieved.

In short, involve pupils in all aspects of the learning, including knowing what they can do and what they need to do next.

LIBRARY

I have always imagined that Paradise will be a kind of library.

Jorge Luis Borges

Public libraries have long provided a local hub for a range of civic services centred on the ideology of free and wide access to books and learning. As well as being a geographical catalyst for book interest and reading for pleasure, libraries represent a quiet haven for many. They inspire curiosity and enquiry-based learning and build independence in young people. Above all, they are a community space.

Sadly, for many, books are simply a luxury rather than a necessity. In recent years, the alarming erosion of local libraries and physical bookshops, along with continued economic pressures in households, has added to the challenge of making books part of children's daily life and engendering a love of books from birth.

The National Literacy Trust's annual book ownership survey shows declining trends (2024d). In 2024, around 1 in 11 people aged between 5 and 18 reported that they did not own a single book. This figure rose to 1 in 8 for children from economically disadvantaged backgrounds, or when the demographic was narrowed to children aged between 5 and 8.

This makes the school library more vital than ever, and yet school libraries are under threat. With competition for space and the pressure of school funds, it can be a challenge to keep a central library going. In 2022, the Book Trust found that 1 in 8 primary schools no longer have a dedicated library space; this figure was as high as 1 in 4 for schools situated in economically deprived areas.

REFRESH BOOK AREAS

While a regular injection of new publications is ideal, there are plenty of ways to regenerate an existing library space without a budget.

Critically examine any book nooks around the school and decide whether they need a facelift. Even if a book corner is seemingly inviting, think about how long it has looked the same. Perhaps its appeal and draw have waned over time and a new dose of interest is needed. Have a termly shake-up to reignite curiosity. Refresh displays of books, posters and resources to stimulate interest. These could take the form of:

- a topical theme such as 'women in science' or 'protecting the environment'
- a feature on a specific author
- some 'Have you read this yet?' books, including recommendations from staff and pupils
- an introduction to new authors and illustrators.

Develop a library environment rich with books and reading materials of all types: graphic novels, modern non-fiction, magazines, picture books (including wordless books), biographies of inspiring people and collections of short stories and poems. Include audio versions of books via tablets and headphones for pupils to follow along with, as well as old favourites and 'quick reads'.

AUDIT BOOK STOCK

Do a periodic stock take. Have some books had their time? Be brave and do a library cull. Rehome any damaged, old-fashioned-looking books. The book covers *will* be judged, and tatty books suggest reading is not valued in the school. Check whether some books – especially non-fiction – are now factually inaccurate. In my first school library, I needed to remove books on space that looked forward to man landing on the Moon! After the spring clean, make a list of what is left and where the gaps are; prioritise these areas using any available budget or when asking for donations.

Curate your remaining collection carefully as an abundance of choice can sometimes be overwhelming. Try rotating the contents of the bookshelves. Less is sometimes more, so consider boxing up some books and then swapping them back in after a term so that pupils see something different. After a while, bring out some of the old favourites and let pupils become reacquainted with them.

Finally, ensure material is not limited to one single scheme; vary the diet by using a variety of publishers with different styles. Provided the progression of phonics is adhered to, you will be able to expand the pupils' diet of decodables for your scheme. Whatever the scheme, allow pupils the chance to take a book home for pleasure – even if they can't read it themselves. If pupils are on a post-phonics reading programme, allow opportunities for free choice: we all want to be able to indulge in a quick read or a re-read from time to time, and there is no need for a book to always be harder and more challenging than the one before.

REPRESENTATION IN LITERATURE

As Dr Rudine Sims Bishop (1990) put it so beautifully:

> Books are sometimes windows, offering views of worlds that may be real or imagined, familiar or strange. These windows are also sliding glass doors, and readers have only to walk through in imagination to become part of whatever world has been created or recreated by the author. When lighting conditions are just right, however, a window can also be a mirror.

Review library shelves and school reading spines to ensure books and literary experiences give children the windows, mirrors and doors they need to see themselves represented and understand the diverse nature of our society. Do they have access to a wide range of quality literature that features characters from diverse families, socioeconomic backgrounds, cultures and ethnicities operating in diverse settings? Do children meet characters with different disabilities and identities?

Regardless of the make-up of your school community, representation matters.

Schools prepare students to be tolerant, respectful members of society and this begins with a fuller understanding of the wider world in which they live. In our global, often fractious society, it is more important than ever that we build empathy and tolerance. A diverse diet in literature is a powerful piece of that puzzle. Include children in school book choices. Who would they like to see on their bookshelf? Are their own lived experiences represented in your school's book spine? Are there cultures or individuals of whom they would like a better understanding?

As you conduct your library audit, dig deeper to check the nature of the representation. Ensure that the characters are authentic and fully fleshed out with agency in their story, rather than tokenistic, one-dimensional additions who could be easily swapped for someone else without affecting the plot.

The annual Centre for Literacy in Primary Education (CLPE) report *'Reflecting realities'* (2024) presents the conclusions of research into ethnic representation and diversity in children's literature. The most recent study shows that, while children's publishing has moved forward since the first report in 2017, when only 4% of children's books featured racially minoritised characters, there is still a long way to go. When the 30% figure of 2022 was placed under scrutiny, it was found that the characters portrayed were often thinly sketched with little or no ability to shape the narrative.

Use reports such as these, and booklists such as Lit in Colour from Puffin (https://litincolour.penguin.co.uk/), to ensure that limited budgets reach the best books on offer in terms of representation in literature.

Consider the scenarios and themes within the books to ensure that they are not weighted towards war, refugeeism, bullying or racism. Look for books that offer positive situations and representations or where a person's identity, while intrinsically relevant, is not the main theme of the book. Allow pupils to see that people of all backgrounds experience similar desires and dreams, fears and failures, and help them to connect to familiar themes and goals. Provide non-fiction books that celebrate the contribution of black scientists, athletes with disabilities or gay artists, for example.

Vitally, examine authorship to check that you have a range of writers represented. For generations, libraries were filled with the works of white, male authors because of the limited opportunities for anyone else to be published. Without putting aside the 'must-read' ancient and modern classics, seek to build in the voices of people of all genders, cultures and ethnicities across both fiction and non-fiction.

Your library should portray authentic representations and lived experiences of all authors and illustrators, including people of colour, marginalised communities (such as Travellers or First Nations people), and people experiencing physical disabilities or neurodiversity. Not only do the contents of a book matter, but all children deserve to see themselves represented on the cover. At the very least, this builds a culture of belonging, but hopefully too the inspiration and empowerment to believe that their written voice matters.

SUPPORT BOOK SELECTION

When I chat to pupils in schools, I find that it is rare – even if they enjoy books – that they can reel off the names of more than three or four authors. And yet many book corners are still traditionally laid out spine to spine by author name. This can lead to pupils aimlessly pulling out books and staring at the covers, none the wiser. Instead, consider organising books in collections and with the cover facing out on the bookshelf. Try these ideas to inspire children as they browse:

- baskets of books labelled by genre or themes such as 'friendship' or 'sport'
- books labelled with a message such as, 'If you laughed at *Dogman* by Dav Pilkey, you might also enjoy this' or 'Once you have read *The Boy at The Back of the Class* by Onjali Q. Raúf, you could try this next'
- sticky notes placed at an exciting point in a book; the children can dip in and see whether they are intrigued to read more
- a list of top 20 books recommended by the previous class. At the end of the year, pupils can revisit it and see which titles on the list they agree with, as well as make their own list for the incoming class.

Support pupils to understand the layout of the non-fiction space by teaching them how to use the Dewey Decimal System. It is the universal organisation method for libraries and makes for efficient browsing and returning of books. Ensure the guide is prominently displayed and available for reference, and consider facilitating pupils' navigation of the system by minimising the number of decimal places used and backing this up with with colour-coded stickers for each broad section.

USE THE LIBRARY WELL

Build in time for visits to the central library space. If left to chance, not all pupils will opt to use it, especially if there is a reasonably well-stocked class book corner. Each class could have a timetabled library slot, and a whole reading lesson could be held there during that rotation, if space allows.

A library visit is a great opportunity for research as well as personal browsing. With so many non-fiction books on offer, consider a teaching session on note-taking or book navigation through use of contents pages, index pages and glossaries. Younger children especially will find it a lot easier to browse books than the internet. Don't forget that some children find non-fiction more engaging than stories, so ensure they have the chance to take these home too.

Be creative and flexible in your timetabling design. Pupils could be encouraged to use the library as a quiet space during breaktime sessions. As well as opportunities for browsing books, activities such as board games or read-aloud sessions could be a feature. Foster community spirit by appointing peer librarians alongside a member of support staff to keep charge. With careful managing, the library could also be open before and after school for children to visit with carers or as part of wrap-around school care. It could even host breakfast reading clubs or end-of-day drop-everything-and-read sessions.

To make the very best use of your school library, do reach out to professionals. The School Library Association provides a wealth of advice and support for library design, book curation and training. You could also consult your local Schools Library Service. There are many ways to join forces to get the most out of the school and public spaces, especially during the school holidays.

> **ASIDE**
>
> **BOOK CARE**
>
> From the outset, children should be encouraged to respect books and treat them with care. Teach them how to handle the pages carefully, not to bend or tear pages or leave them lying around where they could get damaged. Books are expensive to replace, and children need to see them as a revered resource rather than a disposable commodity.
>
> For library sessions, provide each pupil with a name card; this needs to be the length of A4 and reinforced. The children can decorate and personalise these. When they browse, they must insert their card marker into the place from which they take a book. When they are finished with the book, they return it to where their marker is. This prevents chaos at the end of a library session.
>
> It is easy to underestimate the amount of time and effort needed to look after a library area, but it's essential if pupils are to get the most out of this valuable school resource. Appoint pupil librarians on a rotation, whose role it is to do final check of the space at the end of a session and encourage other children to put everything back in place.

MODELLING

In teaching it is the method and not the content that is the message.

Ashley Montagu

We cannot learn in a vacuum. Humans have an innate desire to model their behaviours, language and even thoughts on those they observe around them, and this is especially true of the most impressionable in our society: children. Research by Albert Bandura (1977) emphasised the role of social interactions in children's learning. Some children do seem to simply osmose the learning, mimicking speech and language structures with ease and emulating reading and writing patterns by watching.

More often, pupils will need explicit models for each separate skill and each step of the process. When we provide clear models, scaffold learning appropriately and gradually remove this support, we create independent learners who can reconstruct skills with confidence. Modelling the desired learning is a cornerstone of effective pedagogy, and teachers do it all day long, demonstrating everything from how to throw and catch, to how to build a clay pot or carry out a mathematical operation.

Explicit modelling is not always robust in English lessons. This is due in part to an assumption that once pupils have mastered the basic skills in oracy, reading and writing, they will transfer them automatically to the next stage. It is obvious to us that building a coil pot from clay will be unfamiliar to pupils and so will need careful explanation and guided practice. But when it comes to modelling the language that pupils are already employing with ease, how do we decide where to build from? And, more challenging still, how do we make those invisible processes *visible*?

STAGES OF WRITING

Each stage of the writing process needs its own careful modelling. Regularly demonstrate how to:

- note-take without copying chunks
- gather ideas and plan the overall structure and content
- adhere to a specific format such as the layout of a poem or clear sections of a report
- draft and craft their writing
- review, evaluate and edit their final piece
- proofread and publish for their audience.

INDEPENDENT WRITING

Extended writing needs extensive modelling to give pupils the confidence to work independently. The practice of sharing prepared slides or photocopies of a complete text puts the modelling process at risk. I often see instances where pupils are presented with a pre-written model to read through and a list of success criteria. There is then an expectation that they will magically recreate something similar. This is akin to showing children a beautifully iced cake along with a recipe and asking them to deliver their own exquisite patisserie. Children need to see the steps along the way; how did you get to that stage?

However, simply modelling live, sentence by sentence, is also of limited value. Pupils are now watching the equivalent of a baking show with the sound turned off. Less-confident children will be left with no choice but to 'hug the model' – produce a near replica of your example. The added ingredient is live commentary. In the same way as a celebrity chef will explain that 'a splash of vinegar will counteract the sweetness of a sauce' or 'folding the mixture will retain the air bubbles', modelled writing needs an explanation behind each language choice. How have you constructed that sentence and why does that make it accurate and effective?

Similarly, supporting pupils to orally rehearse and internalise a set piece provides for limited innovation unless there is a further piece of work to explain how the sentences have been constructed and how they could

MODELLING

be manipulated. Without that, you simply have rote learning without metacognition and the pupils will have no idea how to adapt.

In his 2012 article 'Principles of instruction', Barak Rosenshine presents modelling as one of the key principles of instruction but stresses the importance of revealing the construction processes of the worked example by thinking aloud while demonstrating. This supports pupils to focus on specific steps of a task and empowers them to replicate them.

In the construction of writing, teachers need to be explicit about the language choices they are making: how to employ language features accurately and to best effect. Detailed commentary takes time, and it can overload the learner if not used judiciously. Consider Rosenshine's second principle of presenting new material in small steps to avoid overloading working memory.

Look at this example of a concluding paragraph on the life of Mary Anning. It explains the what, the why and the how, but a wise teacher wouldn't want to go beyond three or four sentences before sending pupils off to put example into practice.

model
Mary Anning never lost her interest in curios. She constantly combed her local beach for fossils and dinosaur bones, which she sold to rich London collectors. Inevitably, they claimed these finds as their own.

commentate
This paragraph brings the reader towards the end of my biography, so I want to say what happened after her biggest find. I'll begin with a sentence linked to the last line of the previous paragraph, which was about all her amazing discoveries. Capital letters for names, of course.

I'll echo that first sentence in my next by saying that she constantly combed the beach for fossils and dinosaur bones (combed has a 'silent' b like *thumb* and *lamb*).

I could start a new sentence: *She sold them to collectors*. Actually, I'll extend the original sentence and add a relative clause to link the information more closely and concisely: the word *which* relates to the fossils and bones.

The collectors would claim the finds as theirs because Mary was a poor woman, so I will start the next sentence with a fronted adverbial – *inevitably* – meaning 'of course this would happen'. If I lead with this word, the reader will see its importance in the sentence as well as how it links to the sentence before; I need a comma after it to indicate a pause before reading the rest of the clause.

Let's read the whole piece back and check. Can you add a final sentence to my paragraph? I'll write one too. (*Because of this, it took many years for the public to know of Anning's contribution to palaeontology.*)

Modelling a concluding paragraph.

Unless you are a supremely confident and experienced writer, it is unlikely that you will be able to compose the perfect extended model on the go. You'll want to demonstrate a fine balance of skills, at a pitch that simultaneously delivers challenge and support while engaging and inspiring your reader.

The trick is to pre-prepare a carefully crafted model along with annotations for commentary and present it as though you are composing as you go. Keep it by you and refer to it by all means, but the pupils need to believe that you are modelling the creative process that they are expected to undergo, rather than revealing a fait accompli.

Modelling writing is a form of learning scaffolding: effective modelling is verbal, visual, replicable and temporary. And, like any structural scaffolding on a construction site, support in school should be gradually removed as learning construction is completed. A successful session of modelling extended writing should allow for innovation and dynamism, but if it remains revealed throughout the lesson, the temptation for pupils will be to rely on it too extensively.

Modelling is most effective when pupils learn not to mirror or imitate but to assimilate general rules and transferable skills that can add to their knowledge schema and apply to different scenarios. After modelling, remind the pupils what you have done to craft your writing and offer prompts before removing the model altogether:

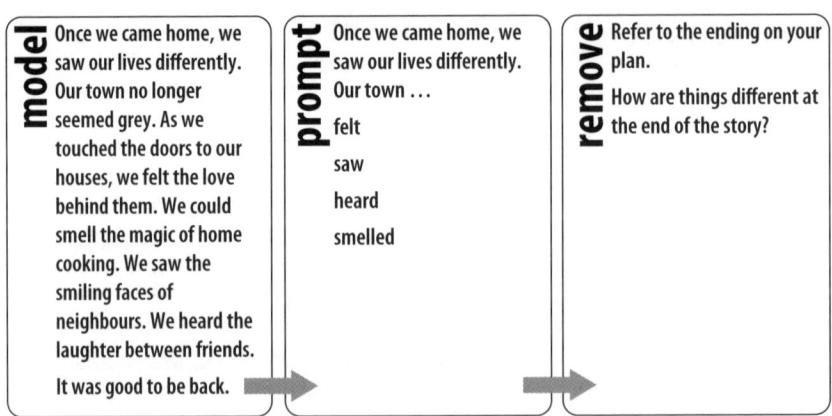

The model should be removed to avoid pupils relying on it too extensively.

COGNITIVE LOAD

When modelling writing, decide in advance which aspects of the text you would like to draw attention to, which skills you'll be commentating on and how much you intend to demonstrate. Layer in the learning: include brief nods to familiar learning, explicit reminders of recently taught skills and a heavy focus on new concepts being demonstrated in context.

If you model sentence upon sentence, or attempt to reveal the entire text in one go, you not only risk overloading the pupils with multiple skills, but you'll begin to lose their attention. Just as you would with a small, guided group, move between 'I do', 'we do' and 'you do'.

If 'I do' is modelled writing, 'we do' is 'shared' writing. This could involve the pupils contributing to the next part of your model by suggesting words that could slot into a sentence, practising spelling a word you'd like to use on their whiteboard or supplying the last sentence in your paragraph.

Before sending pupils off for their independent application, give them a summary of what you did and a few prompts to remind them what they need to do, and refer them to their plan, so they don't copy your model but innovate it to fit their original idea. Once they have had suitable time to write a section independently, bring the pupils back for the next piece of modelling.

ADAPTIVE TEACHING

Use assessment for learning to respond to the needs of the pupils during the session, whether that be adjusting the pitch and pace of the modelled instruction, or making adjustments in terms of support or challenge for groups or individuals. Perhaps pupils have not demonstrated a desired skill during the first part of the lesson and further exemplification is needed. Live modelling – unlike a pre-prepared model – can be reworked as you go.

Watch pupils' behaviour and responses during modelling; some children might benefit from being released from a whole-class instruction to begin their independent work, allowing you to repeat or reinforce exemplification for others.

English as a subject is complex and comprises several interlinked yet individual disciplines. Within each area of learning, modelling will take on different guises for different skills. At times, whole-class modelling is necessary, but on occasion, you will need to swoop in and support less confident learners individually. Compare the following examples:

Handwriting

- supporting pupils to hold various media for writing and sit appropriately
- demonstrating letter formation by articulating the strokes needed as you perform the movement
- providing instruction on joining letters and maintaining consistency in handwriting.

Reading

- scooping up separate words into phrases and sentences to derive meaning
- reading with expert prosody and inviting the pupils to read back with the same intonation and expression
- using strategies such as skimming and scanning, or discovering the meaning of unfamiliar words.

Oracy

- providing example answers: an oral scaffold that can be adapted to give a similar response
- rehearsing a given sentence structure ready for application in writing
- demonstrating effective public-speaking skills.

Spelling

- use of a scaffold – for example, how to interact with a phoneme mat or build words in a phoneme frame
- strategies for spelling, such as segmenting words into syllables or following a procedure for 'chop, change or doubling' before a suffix
- techniques that support remembering and checking spellings.

DEVELOPING SELF-REGULATION

By making abstract concepts and skills tangible, modelling enhances pupils' comprehension in reading and their understanding of the craft behind effective communication in English.

Yet those models are not a means of transferring knowledge but of developing skills. Psychologist Lev S. Vygotsky (1978) stressed: 'The teacher must adopt the role of facilitator not content provider.' As we guide pupils through that zone of proximal development, explicit modelling is the gateway to independence and the goal is to remove its requirement.

Model self-regulation skills as part of daily instruction: suggest strategies, provide frequent opportunities to practise, and scaffold to allow pupils to support themselves. This is the aim of all modelled practice: developing the metacognition behind the learning so that pupils can apply it, monitor their own progress and self-scaffold when needed.

ASIDE

BOOKS AS MODELS FOR WRITING

From our earliest days, our language development is based upon mimicry. We copy the noises, words and communicative gestures of others in order to be like them, to fit in and to be able to respond. As well as directly copying language patterns for our own use, we can refine and enhance our range by taking words or phrases that we like the sound of and incorporating them into our repertoire.

Educational trainer and author Pie Corbett popularised the term 'magpieing' to describe and encourage this practice. Magpies are intelligent birds who have a habit of taking and hoarding random objects for their own gain. They are famously attracted to shiny objects, and Pie urges children to pick shiny words and phrases to adorn their spoken language and writing.

Quality texts, chosen for their literary craft, provide the perfect model for pupils' writing. Acquiring language from what we read will often happen quite subconsciously. But from an educational perspective, explicitly teaching children to notice the gems that can be repurposed is more effective, more systematic. Support them to draw inspiration from the text: collect versatile phrases, metaphors that can be applied in many contexts, words that have multiple nuanced meanings.

And let's not beat around the bush here – we are not simply borrowing words and phrases for creative gains. We don't intend to give these words back. We want to create kleptocrats: people who make themselves rich and powerful by stealing from others. And we need the language acquisition to be internalised and become part of a permanent repertoire, not simply one that evaporates when it is no longer word of the week.

By the end of KS2, pupils should be writing effectively for a range of purposes and audiences. Strong models provided by teachers will support generic construction, but confident writers will begin to emulate the style and writerly craft of established authors, poets and journalists. To be judged as working at the 'greater depth standard', a pupil needs to demonstrate that they are 'drawing independently on what they have read as models for their own writing (e.g literary language, characterisation, structure)' (Standards & Testing Agency, 2018).

NETWORKS

When we have any function, whether it's language or vision or cognitive functions like memory, we aren't dealing with a straight line to the brain that says, 'This is what I do.' The brain builds a network of connections, a network of neurons that have a particular role in that function.

Maryanne Wolf

The *Oxford English Dictionary* contains over half a million words. Even the most industrious pupil would struggle to learn the meaning or spelling of each of these words individually.

Researchers have struggled to quantify exact vocabulary size, but various estimates suggest that adult native speakers typically know an incredible 15,000 to 20,000 word families (i.e. root words and their derivatives). How does the human mind have capacity for such a vast store? The answer is undoubtedly to do with schemata.

A schema is a mental filing cabinet or a structure that helps the learner process, connect and organise new information. Rather than storing thousands of random pieces of learning separately, the brain attempts to link a new piece of knowledge with one that is already known. It then files it with the linked information. When a child learns a new dinosaur name, for example, the mind instantly starts making links between this and other, more familiar dinosaurs, firing up visual images and fascinating facts.

As long as there is already a file marked 'dinosaur' in the brain, the learner has context and understanding upon which to build new learning. If no folder exists, the learner needs to create a new one, which will be a subfolder of 'creatures'.

Ofsted's January 2019 update explains: 'It is unhelpful to think of pupils' minds as "empty vessels" waiting to be filled with isolated, disconnected pieces of information. People learn new knowledge when new concepts are connected in their minds with what they have already learned.' Much about quite how the brain works remains a mystery, but we do know that the capacity for long-term memory is limitless and schemata, therefore, enable children to move learning from the short-term memory into a more permanent, ordered system that can be called upon whenever needed.

SYSTEMISING SPELLING

Any spelling system is complex and, as we have established, there are many thousands of words to assimilate. For spelling instruction to be successful, the idea of connecting new concepts to old must be harnessed; we must remind pupils of what they already know about a particular convention, pattern or phoneme.

Pupils need to access prior learning, not just for its own sake, but with the express intent of creating a firm foundational knowledge on which to build. We then need to support pupils to use their own burgeoning understanding of word patterns, rules and concepts to help them spell new linked, but hitherto unknown, words. The aim is to give them skills and tools that will allow them independence in word building.

For instance, when teaching pupils that the /dʒ/ phoneme is sometimes spelled 'dge' in words like fudge and dodge, I must first remind them that they already know that 'j' spells /dʒ/ in jam and sometimes /dʒ/ is spelled with a 'g' in words like giant and giraffe. Now I am carefully and deliberately building up a schema in the minds of the pupils, which becomes 'sticky' knowledge that will stay with them in the long term. Drawing on existing knowledge also promotes self-awareness, self-esteem and supports metacognition: 'I know and understand more than I realised!'

It is feasible that pupils who are confident spellers are already adept at creating a spelling schema in their minds. Less confident spellers may need guidance to create that schema. If a pupil is supported to remember overarching conventions pertaining to a spelling objective, they have fewer facts to remember than if they try to remember each word individually.

For example, if pupils are secure with the Year 1 knowledge that the digraph 'oy' is found at the end of words such as *boy* and *toy*, but that the same phoneme is spelled 'oi' when in the middle of a word like *coin* or *boil*, then they can also spell *annoy* or *destroy*, as well as *embroiled* or *boiler*. If a pupil can articulate this knowledge, there is a good chance that they can apply it to unfamiliar words and have a better chance of spelling them correctly.

Word maps are a great way of getting pupils to think about linked learning and making visual connections in the mind. For example, if you know how to spell the word *act*, what else might you be able to spell? If you understand that words where the phoneme 'k' follows a long 'ay' are spelled with a split vowel digraph, -ake, which words can you spell?

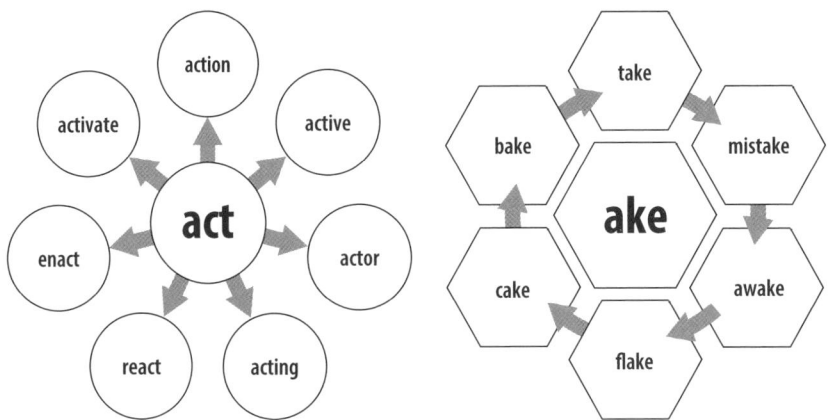

Two different types of word map.

Frequent revision of that pattern is essential to build strong connections in the long-term memory and facilitate recall. Try to move away from teaching pupils to memorise sets of words for spelling tests, and instead move towards teaching them to internalise and understand the key principles of the spelling system. Enable them to build words from a knowledge of how to do so, rather than attempting to draw from a list of potentially irrelevant words that will soon evaporate from the short-term memory.

The true value of spelling instruction is whether pupils can apply their learning in context, especially in their independent writing. Once pupils have established a set of spelling networks in their mind, there is a greater chance that they can write with transcriptional fluency and monitor the accuracy of their orthographical choices.

DICTATION

Dictation is a useful way of checking whether the pupils have taken away a principle for spelling many words rather than a memory trick for one word. The tight framework also means that they can focus on application of the new spelling pattern without having to consider compositional skills.

Returning to an earlier example: you have now taught pupils that the grapheme 'dge' appears at the end of a syllable and after a single vowel, making a short vowel sound. You modelled words like *fridge* and *budge*. A quick dictation using similar words will show whether they have internalised this convention:

The badger lives in a set by the hedge.

We dodged a car on the bridge.

Of course, with the focus moved away from composition, cognitive load is also freed up for checking the application of basic punctuation and concentrating on accurate letter formation. Pupils could then be challenged to make up their own short sentences including any of the words they have been learning, further securing those new networks.

MAPPING OUT WRITING

Pupils need to be able to simultaneously juggle multiple skills when crafting their writing. Because the brain processes visual and verbal information separately, dual coding can help pupils understand and retain more information than if it were simply written down. Visual scaffolds that are commonly employed with younger pupils are often absent in KS2 classes and yet these prompts work wonders for creating networks in the mind. The following three ideas are adaptable to any scenario and should be part of every teacher's toolkit.

Story maps

These prompts help to visually block a narrative into a summarised, ordered version of the text. Pupils can rehearse the story using the images as prompts that help them to internalise the stages. Word prompts could be added for older pupils. As they retell the story, children are increasingly able to flesh out the map by adding details.

An example of a story map.

Spider diagrams

A centralised idea spins out into a web of connected detail, with pupils adding information to their own or a shared knowledge organiser. If the details are placed under thematic headings on the diagram, these can become individual paragraphs ready for writing. Alternatively, they can be used summatively so that pupils can record what they have learned.

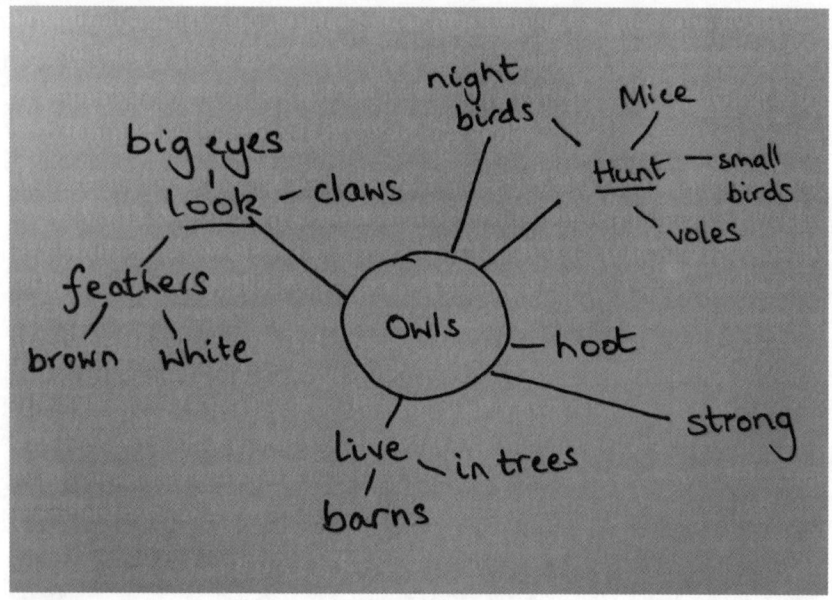

A spider diagram for a piece of writing about owls.

Skeleton frames

These were devised by Sue Palmer as a way of supporting children to plan their ideas and organise their writing coherently. Different writing genres take different shapes, and each skeleton is set out in a way that supports the writer to understand the different genre structures. The bare skeletons themselves are a great memory jogger, but the pupils can plan their writing in this format and add content to the bare bones.

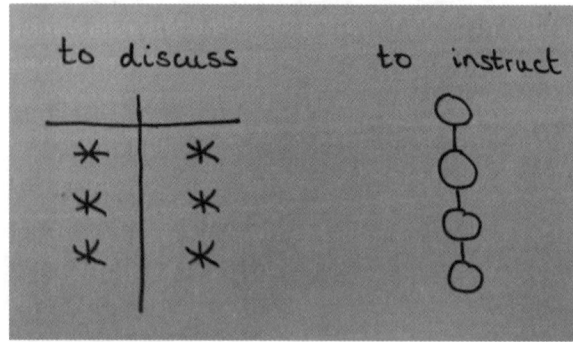

A skeleton frame.

PRE-TEACHING

Before any lesson, consider the pupils' starting points. Ascertain, through formative assessment, what prior knowledge and skills (as well as misunderstandings) children bring with them to the lesson, and select those with potential gaps in learning who would benefit from a quick session of pre-teaching.

While all lessons should begin with an opportunity to re-ignite prior learning and fire synapses ready to take on new learning, some pupils may benefit from a quick session even before that. Pre-teaching is a vital way of scaffolding learning so that all pupils can start the main session with confidence and are able to be successful during the lesson. Use these mini-sessions to address misconceptions, fill in gaps and praise successes.

This could take the form of:

- reading a text that the class are about to meet for the first time to allow for better comprehension on the next read
- walking through a story from the previous day to re-establish the order of events
- exploring key vocabulary that might be needed but that the pupil may not know
- discussing some concepts that the pupil may have less experience of than others
- connecting to the pupil's background knowledge, thus preparing to create networks to the new learning
- supporting the pupil to list what they already know or can remember about the learning to build self-esteem
- orally rehearsing sentence structures that the pupil might wish to employ in their writing.

A well-designed curriculum acknowledges the interconnectedness of the English disciplines and provides opportunities for pupils to build understanding of core concepts across them. Teachers make explicit the links between vocabulary, reading, writing, spelling and oracy; they help pupils to piece their understanding together and build a central body of sequenced learning.

A growing body of new concepts is underpinned by prior knowledge until pupils have at their disposal an entire network of linked learning on which they can draw with confidence.

> **ASIDE**
>
> This chapter has focused on the importance of supporting pupils to build networks in their own minds, on their own. Children also learn effectively when they collaborate with their peers. Provide networking opportunities for pupils to share their discoveries with each other and consolidate learning, before reporting back to the class:
>
> - Talk partners: Give pupils time to share thoughts and test out ideas in pairs. Promote active listening by inviting pupils to report back what their partner has said.
> - Envoying: Groups of pupils research a topic, record their findings on a large sheet and send an envoy to share with other groups, who add new information.
> - Jigsawing: Groups or individuals research specific parts of a topic, then take turns presenting to form a complete picture. Full reports are shared at the end.
> - Snowballing: Pupils research an area, then circulate and share one fact with each peer, building collective knowledge on the topic.

ORACY

Reading and writing float on a sea of talk.

James Britton

In 1965, Andrew Wilkinson introduced the term *oracy*, noting the neglect of spoken language in education. Since then, efforts have aimed to place oracy on a par with literacy and numeracy. A seminal work by Barnes, Britton and Rosen (1971) established oracy as essential for learning and academic success. However, even decades later, many schools struggle to implement a consistent oracy curriculum.

Criticisms persist: spoken language remains undervalued, curricula lack structure, and planning for oracy skills is weak. Teacher-centred lessons often dominate, and emphasis on standard English can alienate some students. Foundational oracy skills, crucial for development, continue to be overlooked.

In the academic year 2023-24, one in five children nationally failed to reach the expected level for communication and language by the end of their Reception year (Gov.UK, 2024). The Covid-19 pandemic exacerbated the issue. Lockdowns meant limited opportunities for under-fives to socialise at a vital stage of language development. Studies often cite the direct correlation between the amount of direct talk pre-schoolers experience and their success in learning to read.

While oracy is explicitly mentioned in the 2014 national curriculum, the outline for the statutory requirements in spoken language progression for the entire primary phase amounts to a little over one page. Quite a stark contrast when compared to the detail for reading, writing or even spelling. The disparity of provision across the country – along with the lack of certainty and consensus around what strong oracy provision should entail – suggests that the document is not sufficiently detailed in this area.

In 2015, Voice 21 was established to focus research on oracy education and improve access to good-quality provision. The awareness that confident spoken language skills help to narrow the attainment gap among economically disadvantaged pupils has also put oracy on the political agenda.

Increased focus and sustained work have meant that over the last decade, some schools have developed a clearly defined, fully fleshed-out oracy curriculum in which learning to talk, about talk and through talk is integral to all aspects of school life. There are many exemplary schools and trusts with a declared mission to improve pupils' oracy skills, where pupils are confident, articulate and the impact on their academic success can be measured. Such schools often become beacons for other schools looking to replicate that success.

In March 2024, an independent Oracy Education Commission was established in the UK, in recognition of the urgent need to re-establish the entitlement to quality oracy provision for children across all key stages. Chaired by Geoff Barton, the aim was to create a roadmap for an effective oracy curriculum – an opportunity to prioritise oracy development for all children and young people. One of the missions of the organisation, as given on their website, is: 'Define the vision, values and intent of oracy education as part of a broad and enriching education.'

Extensive rounds of research culminated in the release of a final report, *We Need to Talk*, in October 2024.

The commission agreed a definition of oracy as: 'Articulating ideas, developing understanding and engaging with others through speaking, listening and communication.'

It concluded that:

> Oracy is intrinsic to children's early development, to the testing of thought, to social and emotional well-being, to confidence, agency and the ability to challenge or debate important issues in civil and constructive ways.

Given the consensus around the value of spoken language skills in the classroom, it is imperative teachers receive initial training and continued professional development time dedicated to supporting subject knowledge and pedagogy around oracy. This should include training on how we can best understand and support all pupils, but especially those with additional needs. School leaders should evaluate the interventions and strategies that are in place for pupils with delayed language acquisition or those new to English.

Teachers also need to consider how far they are fostering a universal sense of belonging regardless of how pupils speak. They need to feel that their contributions are valid, no matter their dialect, accent or register. Special care should be taken to identify the introverted pupils who rarely volunteer their voice. Observations show that these are the children who experience the fewest adult interactions in school and who get overshadowed in conversations with peers. What opportunities are afforded them to develop their confidence to speak aloud and rehearse oracy skills? It is vital that schools and settings provide a safe space for pupils to practise their skills, and praise contributions in order to build self-esteem and self-efficacy.

It is generally accepted that an oracy curriculum should comprise two pedagogical strands:

1. **oracy education**: supporting pupils to learn *to* talk
2. **dialogic teaching**: teaching pupils how to employ spoken language skills to learn *through* talk.

The Oracy Education Commission report (2024) proposes a third strand: learning *about* talk, in order to develop an awareness of the different contexts of spoken language.

An oracy curriculum should carefully map out the progression of pupils' oracy skills over time. Beyond the early learning goals and teacher observations, there is no further measure of children's communication skills.

Schools might consider implementing an effective and engaging oracy curriculum, comprised of the following strands.

LEARNING TO TALK, LISTEN AND COMMUNICATE

This strand is about developing learning on how to use spoken language effectively. Support pupils to actively listen as well as to understand how and when to talk. Initially, pupils may only feel able to converse with peers or adults on a one-to-one basis, but gradually they can become actively involved in groups and classroom discussion. For some children, speaking out in front of others can be overwhelming; it is, therefore, important for teachers to consider the social and emotional aspects of speaking.

Pupils should be taught to articulate their thoughts clearly in full sentences. They should learn different sentence types such as statements, questions, commands and exclamations. Teachers need to model effective, accurate clause structure. Use speaking frames that give pupils a scaffold onto which they can build their response. These can take the form of brief spoken guidance or even written prompts at the point of asking a question. For example:

Please begin your answer like this: The book is exciting because …/In my opinion …/Not only should they … but they must also …

Pupils who are new to English will need careful and structured support to acquire the language, and modelled examples that can be replicated provide a beneficial approach to that. Receptive language will generally outpace productive language so pupils may understand more than they feel confident to say. At times, the vocabulary is there but understanding how to manipulate the grammar is a barrier. Pre-teaching useful phrases and sentence structures that might support pupils in a lesson could build security.

LEARNING THROUGH TALK, LISTENING AND COMMUNICATION

This is also known as dialogic teaching. Through exploratory talk, pupils build their knowledge and understanding across the curriculum.

The use of varied partner and group discussion is a crucial means whereby pupils can tentatively probe and deepen their understanding of concepts and viewpoints before writing. Pupils should be taught to evaluate contributions, discern useful information and participate in activities like debates, interviews and presentations. Dialogic teaching allows teachers to guide classroom discussions to enrich students' understanding.

In a dialogic reading session, high-quality book talk encourages pupils to articulate their ideas, build on those of their peers and engage in skills such as questioning, clarifying and arguing to solidify their knowledge across all subjects. In our ever-more-polarised world, it is vital that pupils learn empathy, tolerance of other viewpoints and to listen to the experiences of others.

Just as book talk helps the reader develop their comprehension of a text, discussion of writing also affords the opportunity to clarify thoughts. It is vital that pupils articulate their ideas and collaborate at every stage of the process. The Year 1 Programme of Study (DfE, 2013a) explicitly requires that pupils be taught to write sentences by:

- saying out loud what they are going to write about
- composing a sentence orally before writing it.

This principle should be woven in from this point onwards.

Whether in English lessons or across the curriculum, supply pupils with technical vocabulary and definitions, and model usage so they can use specific terminology to build learning. Model use of grammatical structures that pupils can rehearse orally before employing target language in their own writing. The language of writing tends to be more formal, structurally complex and rich in literary devices than spoken language, so pupils need plenty of opportunities to practise what they want to write and verbally draft ideas before committing pen to paper.

LEARNING ABOUT TALK, LISTENING AND COMMUNICATION

Learning about talk, listening and communication is about studying the art of communication and building knowledge of spoken language in its many contexts. It includes understanding how to clearly and effectively communicate a point of view as well as how to listen respectfully to those of others. Neil Mercer (n.d.) notes the importance of embedding 'ground rules for oracy'. For many, including those with special educational needs, specific support with the social and emotional aspects of talking may be required.

Consider how you will establish ground rules for speaking and listening with pupils who haven't mastered the cognitive elements of their own role in social interactions. For example, do they understand the importance of turn-taking in discussion and can they self-regulate to avoid interrupting others? Do they know when it is best not to speak at all? Some pupils might struggle with non-verbal cues, such as tone of voice, volume, pitch, pauses, body language and personal space. These skills can be developed through interventions, including use of 'social stories'. These work through model scenarios so that pupils develop conversational skills and learn how to respond in given situations.

The art of rhetoric in state schools has been relatively overlooked compared to the emphasis it receives in the private sector. Ensure your curriculum plots in opportunities for pupils to learn how to speak for different occasions.

Teach them the vocabulary and grammar to use in different genres of spoken language. For example, when composing persuasive speech, model the use of repetition, rhetorical questions and emotive language. Show pupils high-quality examples so that they can evaluate the power of those persuasive language structures. Contrast that with the skills of debating or reporting and support pupils to see the different devices employed.

PERFORMANCE

Learning about talk also involves understanding the art of polished performance or presentation to a range of audiences and for different purposes.

As well as the specific linguistic elements of spoken language, prosodic elements of voice control such as intonation, tone, volume, pace and pause should be modelled and rehearsed. Build in plenty of opportunities for pupils to perform readings of their own writing and published writing, focusing on their expression, but also learning how to add impact by incorporating movements and gestures that contrast with moments of stillness and silence.

Pupils always benefit from activities that support them to take on a persona as they rehearse language orally. Weave in opportunities to practise speaking in a role in drama lessons, 'hot-seat' a character from a book or employ 'readers' theatre' in a read-aloud session.

Consider holding public-speaking sessions or poetry readings. Even the youngest children can learn how to recite a poem, adding in a stamp for emphasis or a pointed finger for dramatic impact. These sorts of activities support pupils to project their voice effectively – a skill not only necessary for teachers.

THE MORAL IMPERATIVE

Schools need to support pupils' communication skills and design opportunities for talk the moment pupils arrive in the education system. They need to weave oracy through every aspect of the curriculum, to enhance learning and create a life-long interest in talking with others to build knowledge and understanding of the world around us.

The nature of our super-connected yet simultaneously fractured modern society requires that its citizens engage, self-advocate and communicate.

ASIDE

INCLUSION

The conventions of talk can still be woven in for children who cannot communicate through verbal exchange. Turn-taking and other social cues are just as vital when signing, for instance. Consider how to support learning through talk for pupils who do not communicate verbally with others, such as those with selective mutism. Teach inclusivity for all through activities such as learning basic sign language. This is something that should be considered regardless of whether there are deaf children in the class.

Similarly, it can be alienating to be a non-native speaker of English in a classroom environment. Little gestures go a long way to fostering self-esteem and belonging for children with English as an additional language, as well as empathy and appreciation for bilingualism on the part of English speakers. Invite children to teach their peers greetings and simple phrases in their home language so that exchanges in a new language are not one-way experiences.

Look at the section on oracy in Section Two to learn about ideas that can support the more introverted pupils in your class to participate and grow in confidence.

PUNCTUATE

Proper punctuation is both the sign and cause of clear thinking.

Lynne Truss

In the relatively short history of writing, punctuation is a bit of a newcomer. Early Latin texts do not even include spaces between words, and punctuation wasn't broadly used until the arrival of the printing press. In fact, the lack of punctuation in early scripture often led to different interpretations of religious doctrine. Think the famously ambiguous 'Let's eat grandma', but involving biblical comma absenteeism.

In her celebrated book *Eats, Shoots & Leaves* (2009), punctuation guru Lynne Truss talks about the dual function of punctuation. 'Punctuation herds words together, keeps others apart. Punctuation directs you how to read, the way musical notation directs a musician how to play.' These tiny – yet mighty – marks simultaneously frame the grammatical elements of a sentence while also performing a directorial role, guiding the reader in terms of inflection, pauses and pace. Commas, for example, can be seen in Ancient Greek playscripts as a means of influencing the actors' delivery of lines.

In the primary English curriculum, pupils are first introduced to these essential marks as syntactical aids: capital letters and full stops act as gatekeepers to sentence boundaries. Once this becomes familiar, simple elocutionary marks can be taught, starting with the question mark to signify an upturn in the voice denoting the end of a query, and the exclamation mark to denote an emphasised point or strong feeling. And so, the marks are gradually and strategically learned, equipping pupils with a variety of symbols that can help them navigate their reading, and that they can employ in their own writing to guide their reader.

Missing marks, or an overzealous employment of marks, can be a source of frustration for many of us. I know I am not the only punctuation pedant who has been known to smugly share a photo of someone else's writing mishap. Rogue apostrophes are a regular find on shop signs: 'Cat's for sale' and 'Arnolds Diner' are two I recently spotted. I confess I did once get out a black pen and pop in the missing apostrophe on an aeroplane safety notice. Where do these misconceptions arise and how can we prevent early writers from developing them?

Like its transcriptional partner, orthography, punctuation tends to pose less of a problem when reading than with writing. After initial modelling and prompting, most pupils will understand the principle of pausing or performing when they see certain marks. Others take a little longer to see their importance and tend to ignore them unless prompted. Fluency instruction with an emphasis on prosody is effective in this case; pupils need to learn how to use punctuation to help them deliver a meaning-laden read. It's also important to point out punctuation as you read with children: 'Why did the writer use an exclamation mark here?' 'Why is this part in brackets?'

BUILDING ON STRONG FOUNDATIONS

When it comes to writing, the skill of knowing which words to herd together and fence off between marks eludes many a child. In a desperate attempt to exert any sort of pattern or rule, some younger pupils will dutifully pop a full stop at the end of each line of writing or cautiously pepper them between every fifth or sixth word. For so many children, the perpetual conundrum of writing craft is: what actually constitutes a sentence, and how do you know when you have reached the end of one?

Naturally the curriculum progression of punctuation mirrors the introduction of associated grammar, starting with the concept of a single-clause sentence. Initial conversations around full stops and capital letters need to be attempted without going too deeply into technical explanations and grammatical terminology involving clauses, subjects and verbs. Has it got a **who** or **what**? And has it got a *doing* or *being* word to tell us what is happening?

- **a robin** *sings*
- **Sam** *is hot*
- **the ball** *bounced*

If it does have these things, it is a sentence. We should, therefore, start with a capital letter to show where the sentence begins and finish with a full stop to show where it ends:

- **A robin** *sings.*
- **Sam** *is hot.*
- **The ball** *bounced.*

It's helpful to model sentences with a clear pattern so that pupils can begin to spot the syntax of subject plus verb. And it's perfectly acceptable for pupils to begin every sentence in the same way as they learn to manipulate that structure for themselves.

If pupils are encouraged to vary sentence openers before they have internalised the basic rhythm and flow of a sentence, punctuation may go quickly awry. It matters little if, at first, every sentence in a story begins with 'The princess'. That pattern is establishing a grammatical groove, supporting a child to internalise it. Taking time to set the foundations leads to stronger understanding on which to build later.

Draw attention to that simple structure in your models, and return to it whenever new grammar is introduced. This basic clause structure is the foundation stone of all sentences, and pupils need to return to it regularly to reinforce understanding and to enable building from solid foundations. Telling pupils to go back and insert punctuation is to no avail if they do not have a secure concept of what constitutes a sentence.

The fronted adverbial gets a lot of bad press in social media. It is often held up as an example of grammatical madness by curriculum vigilantes who have 'managed to write perfectly well without knowing what a fronted adverbial was, thank you very much'. Personally, I love them. Just used one; use them a lot. In a world of linguistic vaguery, the fronted adverbial offers a straightforward and controllable way to vary sentence starts.

Children tend to be quick to pick up the concept. This is partly because of the uniformity of the process: a word or phrase that you can pop at the beginning of your sentence and delineate with a comma before you revert to the subject–verb pattern.

It is also because they are already familiar with this as a spoken and literary device: *After dinner, you can watch TV. Once upon a time, there was a giant.* And finally, you can literally feel the pause in the sentence that the comma affords. It's unambiguous. One day – wait for it – we'll be millionaires – full stop. It's a teacher's dream: teach the pupils to vary sentence starts without disturbing the established word order. It's a handy bolt-on that enhances the writing. Protesters can complain about whether or not we need to name it, but surely the term is as easy to learn and use as 'comma' and 'full stop'.

COMMA CONFUSION

There are several uses of the comma in the English language but the fronted adverbial is my favourite, followed by the equally neat and unambiguous comma to 'separate words in a list'.

The comma is equally hero and villain in primary education. It is at the root of most pernicious problems in punctuation. Yes, there are conventions around its use including those mentioned earlier, as well as rules around demarcating speech, parenthesising clauses or pausing before question tags. But the comma is the punctuation mark that most commonly straddles grammatical accuracy and stylistic choice. The notorious Oxford comma is a prime example of this; a device that causes literary storms in teacups. Luckily, there is no requirement whatsoever for primary children to be taught this concept.

The comma splice, on the other hand, does need addressing. It is a common occurrence in children's books, but it can be tricky to spot as pupils begin to write multi-clause sentences. Like all punctuation problems, this issue can only be solved by shoring up the grammatical understanding behind it. Pupils need to see that a clause needs a subject and a verb (or verb phase); it represents one single idea.

Once you have stated an idea, you need to bring it to a close with a full stop. Alternatively, you can choose to join ideas and you need something to link them. A comma can't do that sort of heavy lifting, but a conjunction can. Older pupils can be shown how a semicolon can be judiciously used instead of a conjunction.

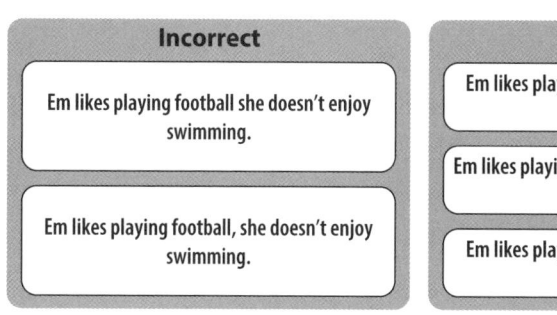
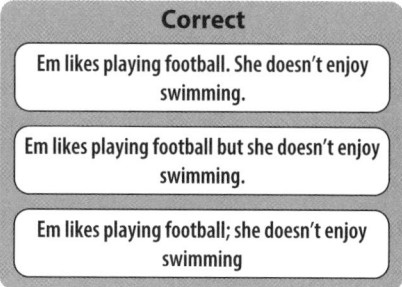

Incorrect	Correct
Em likes playing football she doesn't enjoy swimming.	Em likes playing football. She doesn't enjoy swimming.
Em likes playing football, she doesn't enjoy swimming.	Em likes playing football but she doesn't enjoy swimming.
	Em likes playing football; she doesn't enjoy swimming

FROM AMBIGUITY TO CLARITY

Luckily, the more nuanced aspects of punctuation are introduced as pupils move into upper KS2. Children can be supported to review punctuation choices by reading their writing aloud at the editing stage. As they do so, encourage them to pay close attention to the marks they have – and have not – made. If they paused as they read, did they have the punctuation there to guide their next reader to do the same? If a sentence sounds confusing, do they need to add in any punctuation to parenthesise information or clarify the meaning?

Another way for older pupils to analyse the appropriate punctuation is by setting out sentences in two ways and considering what the punctuation does to the meaning in each case. Compare the following examples:

I enjoy eating, my family and dogs.

I enjoy eating my family and dogs.

Yesterday, there was a man-eating shark at the beach.

Yesterday, there was a man eating shark at the beach.

Mangoes, that grow in hot countries, are incredibly juicy.

Mangoes that grow in hot countries are incredibly juicy.

A similar approach supports pupils to make elocutionary decisions about their own writing. They can compare the effect of the urgency or volume of the following:

Wait until you see this.

Wait until you see this!

And consider the effect on the drama and suspense of long, detailed sentences versus short, snappy ones:

He dashed out onto the alleyway although he had no idea what he should do next. The fog enveloped him and the cold ate into his skin.

He dashed out onto the alleyway. He had no idea what to do next. The fog enveloped him; the cold ate into his skin.

In teaching children punctuation, we equip them with the tools to express themselves clearly and confidently in their writing. Activities like the ones above give pupils the freedom to experiment. Thinking back to the original Ancient Greek marks made to inform actors of how a piece should be read aloud is a great rationale for laying down the principles of punctuation as a foundation for effective communication.

ASIDE

Missing full stops and capital letters are the bane of every primary teacher's life. There are many ways of signposting them. One strategy is to denote a capital letter and a full stop in each sentence with a red pen or pencil. Pupils can replicate this in their own writing: say the sentence, write the sentence, check the sentence. Does it begin and end with a red character? Very quickly, the pairs of red dots followed by capital letters begin to stand out.

Punctuation partners: If a red dot isn't followed by a red capital, it's clear what needs fixing. If there are a few lines of writing without any red pen, it's likely that this section needs checking. The beauty is that, because children are encouraged to say the sentence first, they will naturally plot one idea at a time, and you'll begin to eliminate that stream-of-consciousness effect.

This strategy can work from Year 1 to Year 6 with a few considerations:

- Model and remind pupils of expectations; the routine won't establish itself.
- If the strategy doesn't work (e.g. missing or incorrect plotting of red pencil marks), rewind and reteach the concept of a sentence.
- This only works if you limit the red pencil to the initial and final punctuation. If you start asking pupils to indicate capital letters for names, commas and inverted commas in red, the writing will be littered with distracting marks and the sentence boundaries will no longer be clear.
- Like all scaffolds, this strategy is temporary. If pupils have no problem with this basic punctuation, let them write unhindered.
- With pupils who are writing beyond a paragraph of writing, it is sometimes useful to prompt them to employ the technique just for certain stages: either just the first paragraph to get them into the habit of watching for sentence boundaries, or towards the end when they are running out of stamina and liable to make more mistakes.
- With older pupils, consider temporarily reintroducing the strategy when they have been taught a new grammatical skill. This will help them to maintain control of sentence boundaries even when the clause structure has become more complex.

QUESTION

> Education is not the answer to the question. Education is the means to the answer to all questions.
>
> William Allin

Various research has tried to quantify the volume of questions that teachers ask of pupils. Levin and Long (1981) estimated the figure to be around 300–400 questions per day; Rosenshine (2012) suggested that the most successful teachers might spend, 'up to half the class time lecturing, demonstrating and asking questions'. Regardless of the exact figure, five minutes in any classroom confirms the general idea: questioning is an essential component of a primary teacher's toolkit.

Hattie and Yates (2013) state: 'The teacher's role … is to invite and induce students to engage actively with learning sources.' Much of that engagement has traditionally been fuelled by questioning.

But what makes an effective question? Studies suggest that up to 98% of the questions teachers ask are low level – often closed – and generally ask something the pupil knows the answer to and that can be answered in seconds. But, of course, there is a place for that sort of question in terms of establishing confidence and positivity in the learners, re-igniting existing knowledge and consolidating it through opportunities for spaced recall.

MONITORING UNDERSTANDING

Teachers are well versed in strategies to ensure that all pupils are participating and they have developed myriad ways of asking questions that involve everyone simultaneously. This is especially useful as a means of monitoring understanding.

The teaching of spelling must include opportunities for assessment for learning. Low-stakes recall questions and quizzes are an effective way of checking understanding and building it into the long-term memory. A carefully structured question during a spelling sequence will offer a valuable opportunity to identify any misconceptions while adding to pupils' spelling schema.

Here are a couple of questions relating to a teaching sequence on -cial/-tial word endings that are taught in upper KS2. They aim to fire up connections in the pupils' minds and enable them to make the next step in their learning:

- What do you understand by the following terms: 'root word', 'suffix', 'vowel' and 'consonant'? Tell your partner.
- If the suffix is spelled -cial after a vowel letter, when do you think we might use the spelling -tial?

A spelling test following a teaching sequence only checks whether a set of words is held in a pupil's short-term memory. By contrast, well-crafted questions can assess understanding of concepts applicable to any combinations of words in that set, allowing pupils to apply their knowledge of spelling and vocabulary beyond a short list, whether they have met the words yet or not:

- Can you tell me what the general rule for adding -tial might be?
- On your whiteboard, record the word that you think means: 'relating to the face' (*facial*) and show me. Now show me the word that means 'to do with society' (*social*).
- Can you summarise the two spelling conventions that you have learned today?

Of course, every 'rule' has exceptions and so it is perhaps better to use the term 'convention' when it comes to spelling. But this, in itself, allows for further questioning: 'Can you think of/find any words that don't follow this pattern (such as *financial*)? How might we remember this spelling?' This kind of exploratory question requires pupils to think more deeply about their learning as well as question how they learn best. If they have been well schooled, they will have a variety of strategies they can draw upon.

Some might prefer to come up with a word mnemonic, such as 'financial has a "c", which relates to cash and currency'. Others might prefer visual prompts including colour-blocking the suffix. A few might spot that there is a root word in there that also ends in a 'c' – finance – and this is indeed another convention that holds true for other apparent 'rule-breakers' such as the word *commercial*.

'COMPREHENSION QUESTIONS'

All too often, instructional reading time can become a game of 'guess what's in the teacher's head' as pupils scramble to find the absolute answers to a volley of unilateral questions. Avoid this pitfall by ensuring these sessions involve joint questioning so pupils become used to asking questions as well as answering them. Encourage them to ask their own questions of the text rather than just expecting to answer yours. What would they like to know?

As adult readers, we process the information we read in a variety of ways. Our brains are busy analysing the language, visualising the scene and questioning the information presented to make sense of it. We will undoubtedly adjust our viewpoint and build fuller comprehension as we progress through a text.

Children embarking on their journey from decoding to fluency and comprehension may struggle to understand what others might be doing with such automaticity. They may not even realise that a text should make sense and 'play a movie' in the mind. When teaching pupils *how* to comprehend a text, try to make that invisible process visible. Model how you are piecing together the information by interrogating the text as you go along: 'Why is she opening that door? ... How must she be feeling now? ... What is going to happen to her?'

Model the use of tentative language so that pupils get used to exploring multiple possible answers. Using 'I wonder if ...', 'Could it possibly ...?' or 'Perhaps ...' scaffolds also engenders safety. The 'I'm not sure but we're just sharing possible thoughts' language means that no one will judge and others can add their own possibilities into the mix.

Ensure that every reading session offers pupils the chance to ask their own questions of the text. They could record their understanding in a format like this:

- The 'What do I know?' question tends to elicit the retrieval of information directly from the text.
- The 'What do I think I know?' section requires a bit of inference backed up by evidence.
- By contrast, the 'What do I want to know?' query encourages the pupils to go further in their engagement with the text.

There is no defined answer here, but the enquiry could lead the pupil (and their peers) into an interesting discussion that deepens their understanding of the text.

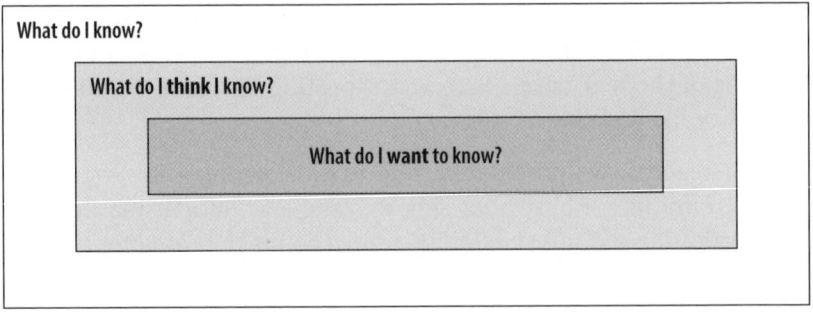

Asking questions of a text.

Similarly, inviting pupils to ask questions directly of their peers (perhaps with older pupils recording these on sticky notes or cards) is an activity that promotes higher-level thinking than is traditionally achieved by the teacher firing a series of questions at the class. Not only does this act presuppose that the pupil must have contemplated the answer to be confident enough to ask, but there is also an element of challenge involved. Pupils tend to enjoy the idea that they might come up with a question to floor their partner, or that they have thought of a question that no one else has considered.

QUESTIONS FOR WRITING

Just as we need to model the process of active reading, we need to develop pupils' ability to craft their own writing by interacting with it. All too often, pupils see the process of writing as a linear journey. They are focused on the end goal of completion but are unaware that a writer must evaluate as they go. If we use cooking as an analogy, you'll recognise that a cook constantly interrogates their own process along the way: 'Do I need more seasoning?', 'Is that baked through, or does it need five more minutes?', 'Will people enjoy eating this?'

In the same way, a writer should aim to question their own writing as they go – monitoring language choices, effectiveness of punctuation and accuracy of sentences towards the end goal of: 'Will people enjoy reading this?' We can also support pupils to evaluate the effectiveness of other people's writing using a similar approach.

Before writing, questions might include:

- Who am I writing for and how do I want to make them feel when they read this?
- What is the purpose of this writing and what are its features?
- What should I include to make my writing effective?

During writing, they should interrogate themselves to make sure they keep their purpose and audience in mind and are aware of other perspectives:

- Would my reader be able to understand what I have written here?
- Will other people consider what I have written offensive or boring?
- If I give this viewpoint, might others disagree?

At the point of editing, they should evaluate their writing, asking questions such as:

- Is there a more precise word I could use here?
- Would an exclamation mark work better here to add emphasis?
- Should I split this into two short sentences for more dramatic effect?

CRITICAL THINKING AND PROBLEM-SOLVING

English is no different from any other curriculum area in that pupils engage more effectively and enhance their knowledge and skills when taught to ask questions about their learning.

Children develop independence, resilience and mental flexibility when they are helped and encouraged to focus on what they can do to support themselves. Those with extensive gaps in learning, especially those who struggle with executive functioning, will often impulsively demand help or suffer lapses in concentration. The ability to problem-solve and self-scaffold when needed is a vital stage of learning.

Model that process explicitly by asking questions that will develop pupils' metacognition, such as: 'Do you know what to do if you get stuck?', 'What do you need to include in this story?', 'How will you know if you have been successful here?' Ultimately, you want these to be internalised by the pupil to become self-prompts that will support their self-regulation skills. Gradually build the repertoire of questions that pupils can ask (and answer) of themselves as they approach a task. These could be grouped under the following headings:

Goal setting and planning:

- How much will I need to write by the end of the lesson?
- Can I try to read this without help?

Getting started/organisation:

- Do I have everything I need to get started?
- What do I need to do first?

Self-monitoring:

- Am I on track to complete this writing?
- Should I check that spelling?

Decision-making:

- Does this word need a capital letter or not?
- Should I start a new line here?

Problem-solving:

- What resource on the table might help me spell this word?
- Which strategy might help me understand this word in the book?

For every question in class, there is a response. Scaffolding responses is useful, especially where pupils still need to develop their spoken language skills:

'Why did you enjoy that story? I might answer like this: I enjoyed that story because it made me laugh. What about you? Start your answer, 'I enjoyed the story because ...'. Think about your response now and practise it in a whisper.'

Sometimes your question might be a disguised command, perhaps in the form of a feedback prompt in a book. Beware of questions that might not get the response you anticipated, such as in this exchange:

T: Can you spot anywhere you might be able to add some adjectives?

P: No.

ASIDE

When designing interactions for a lesson – whether it is questions involving everyone or targeted questions for individuals – it's vital to hold in mind that everyone can find interrogation intimidating at times. You need only watch a game show to see how confident people can crumble under the pressure of the simplest of questions. You yourself may have been through an inspection where the dread of what you might be asked overshadows all else.

Consider how certain questions can be disengaging or feel threatening to certain pupils. Think about students who generally find the classroom environment overwhelming; teacher questioning can instil an extra level of panic.

Certain question styles can be especially off-putting, so use them judiciously.

QUICK-FIRE QUESTIONS

Some pupils need more time to consider their answers. Allow processing time in the following ways:

- Introduce a 'question sandwich': Front-load the question, provide the information and then re-pose the question. 'In a minute I am going to ask you where Matilda was hiding. Right, listen to this part of the story ... OK. Where was Matilda hiding?'
- Allow pupils to make jottings before expecting them to answer.

POUNCE QUESTIONS

Having a 'no-hands-up' rule in class is fine in principle, but it can take away pupils' right to opt out and leave them feeling vulnerable if they don't know the answer. Imagine living in fear of your name being picked out of a pot of lollipop sticks. Consider these options to minimise the worry:

- Use this strategy only when the answer is open enough that no one will feel stuck, for example, 'Who is your favourite character in this story?'
- Employ other ways in which pupils can submit an answer non-verbally, for example, by using a mini-whiteboard.

READING

The more that you read, the more things you will know. The more that you learn, the more places you'll go.

Dr Seuss

The lines above may well be displayed somewhere in your school – above the library door or on the wall of your book corner. They are beloved by teachers because they succinctly sum up the power of books and how vital it is that all children can and do read. Success in reading for meaning is the holy grail of education. All teachers want their pupils to go far, to be transported within the pages of a book and in their life chances. Yet arguably, current curriculum design inhibits academic success for pupils who have poor comprehension skills.

Teaching reading is a complex task, not least because the skills we develop as competent and confident readers can feel tricky to disseminate. There are countless books and papers devoted to the pedagogy of reading, and yet every year around a quarter of all children fail to achieve the national age-related standard for reading comprehension by the time they leave state primary school.

There are several distinct – yet interconnected – skills involved. How do we isolate the individual strands that are tightly woven into that famous Reading Rope, as created by Dr Hollis Scarborough et al. (2001)? For most children, the magic does happen. The threads of reading come together to create a magic carpet that opens up a new world of experiences for them. For others, however, those threads remain stubbornly tangled in a Gordian knot.

By unravelling the rope to explore the components, we can consider how we might re-spin the yarns to teach reading comprehension effectively.

WORD RECOGNITION

There's no two ways about it, pupils must be taught to crack the code. Constant, patient application is the key, as already explored elsewhere in this book. However, automaticity of word reading is only half of the equation. Gough and Tunmer's Simple View of Reading (1986) gives us the formula:

Decoding × Language comprehension = Reading comprehension

Simple activities such as those below require language comprehension as well as decoding ability. The first suggestion relies on an understanding of single-word vocabulary; the second necessitates an understanding of grammar and syntax:

- Read-and-respond instruction cards to show pupils at various points of the day: *pat, sit, wait, clap, jump.*
- Read the caption in the small world area and respond: 'Put the pig on the mat. Is the cat on the bed?'

The skills of decoding and language comprehension need to be taught simultaneously within school, but language awareness will be acquired for most children from birth. In terms of interpreting print, children ideally progress neatly in both aspects and reading comprehension will ensue. But a child who is strong in one skill may not necessarily develop the other with as much ease; some struggle with both sides of the equation. Be aware of where specific difficulties lie and address them systematically.

Good readers know that a text should make complete sense, and they will monitor their own understanding for inconsistencies and errors that impact this. Conversely, some of our weakest readers are unaware that the text should make any sense to them at all. If you've ever sat with a child who carries on undeterred when they misread the word *horse* for *house*, miss a whole line out or turn over two pages at once, you'll recognise a child who is not expecting to derive any meaning from what they are decoding.

Where young children have not realised the relationship between print and meaning, it's fascinating to analyse their answers to simple retrieval questions on a text. If pressed to give an answer rather than 'I don't know', children often give a response based on their own experience without any reference to what has just been read. Language comprehension is there, because they have given you a related answer to their question; they now need to be supported to marry the skills of decoding and reading comprehension. Simple remedies include:

- pausing as the pupil completes a sentence to ask a who, where, what or when question
- asking pupils to tell you something they found out when they read that page
- using prompts such as, 'Put your finger on the bit that tells you the answer'
- supplying an answer and supporting pupils to skim and scan the text to find it, for example, 'The dog's name is Pip. Find the word *Pip*.'

LANGUAGE COMPREHENSION

Language is like a moat running around a castle of comprehension. If a pupil has limited understanding of individual words, phrases or syntax, then the castle drawbridge is up and the portcullis is down. Time is of the essence; children who arrive in school with strong language skills will inevitability cross the moat and enter the castle of reading with greater ease. Scarborough's Reading Rope carves language comprehension into the following areas: vocabulary, verbal reasoning and language structure. We will look at these in turn.

Vocabulary

It's easy to overestimate pupils' vocabulary knowledge, especially when we conclude that just because a child has read words correctly and without hesitation, the words hold meaning for them. All too often we assume a shared understanding of cultural background and experience and fail to address words that are seemingly straightforward.

Children can't possibly learn every word they might meet, nor can they constantly consult a dictionary while reading. We therefore need to give them a range of strategies that they can employ as they read. Vocabulary exploration is an integral component of reading comprehension sessions. Rather than considering 'What does this word mean?', try questions that will act as a bridge to meaning and expand understanding even further:

- 'Find a word that means the same as *sunrise* in this context.'
- Explore language choices that contribute to the whole piece, such as, 'Which words in this passage suggest that Cruella is untrustworthy?'
- Physical responses can demonstrate language comprehension as much as verbal ones. For example: '*Mum was furious with Tom.* Show me a furious face, everyone.' '*Gran sipped her tea.* Let's all sip our tea – what does sipping look like?' Assess based on group response and refine if necessary: '*Furious* means really angry or cross. Let me see your furious faces.' 'Sipping is gentler; we need to take little mouthfuls. Great, now let's gulp our tea.'

Verbal reasoning

There are myriad symbolic words and phrases that can be difficult for pupils to penetrate, especially if they have English as an additional language. Children will meet metaphorical language in everyday expressions, but literary language is awash with imagery and symbolism. Be aware of an assumed knowledge of seemingly obvious similes and metaphors such as 'hard as nails' or 'a blanket of snow'. Idioms can be especially tricky for pupils who struggle to understand beyond the literal. Anticipate phrases like 'someone laughing their head off' or 'crying their eyes out' to avoid anxiety.

As well as employing verbal reasoning skills to analyse metaphorical language, a reader also needs to find clues within the language on the page to infer meaning from what is not directly referenced. We will come back to this in the next chapter.

Language structure

Beyond individual word meaning, the semantics of a phrase, sentence or whole text can be a barrier to comprehension. Pupils need to be taught how words typically combine to create meaning. Where pupils are trying to piece a text together word by word, and are unable to understand phrases or sentences, reading comprehension is negatively impacted. Teachers need to build pupils' understanding of language structures both within and outside of writing sessions to enable fluidity of reading.

As readers, we begin to see grammar in context and note how grammatical constructs can be used by writers to better deliver their message or manipulate the reader's emotions. Analysis of authorial choices (such as use of the passive voice in a formal text or frequent use of expanded noun phrases to set a scene) supports pupils to understand the effect that a writer wanted to have on the reader and can help to build their own writerly knowledge.

Point out punctuation as well as grammar. These marks are unique to reading and form part of the readers' growing concept of print. They are used to support and guide the reader within and across sentences, to denote pauses or add emphasis, and pupils need to be overtly taught to respond to them as they read. Model rise and fall such as, 'Listen how my voice goes up as it reaches the question mark', or 'Can you hear how I paused briefly at the comma?'

Language is complex, but written language gives the intended audience the luxury of lingering to fully digest its use in a way that spoken language does not. Allow time to mull and consider the writer's technique. Did it have the desired effect on you? But beyond a purely literary appreciation and a development of reading comprehension, use reading time to extend pupils' receptive language.

Ultimately, the more they encounter, the more confident they will become to re-use words, phrases and structures in their productive language.

BACKGROUND AND LITERARY KNOWLEDGE

Our knowledge of the world and how it works is crucial to our understanding of what we read. We need a frame of reference to bring to a reading experience, and the less prior knowledge we can connect to, the more impenetrable a text will feel. Life experience is one way of building factual knowledge, conceptual understanding and the associated vocabulary.

But the superpower of books, as Seuss reminds us, is that they are a doorway to other worlds, other lives, other experiences. This can exponentially extend the background knowledge pupils might need and widen their lexicon.

As well as building world knowledge that will support pupils' reading, increasing reading mileage builds knowledge of how literary language works. For our youngest readers, it begins with a fundamental understanding of which way up to hold the book and which way the print flows. They will discover that the written information has a beginning and end, and they can begin to expect certain principles to be followed within the exposition.

Understanding how texts are structured allows a reader to better follow an author's argument or narrative flow. Even where a setting or scenario in a fictional piece is new to a reader, there will be recognisable themes and conventions such as a main character, good versus evil, a quest, a 'happy ever after'. Non-fiction writing will contain genre-specific structures that help readers to navigate the text, even where the subject matter is unfamiliar. Where background knowledge is limited, other prior knowledge can bridge the gap. If pupils can compare with other books they have read, they can make assumptions and predictions based on common themes and patterns.

ASIDE

PITCH

The skills that children bring to bear when reading do not vary hugely from one year to the next. In a nutshell, children need to be able to decode a text fluently and show their understanding; the variable is simply the *pitch* of the text. To be reading at an age-related standard, pupils need to be able to answer questions on a text of an appropriate level of difficulty. So, from initial decodable books to novels from the library, it is vital that books are well matched to the current reading attainment of the pupil so they can successfully comprehend what they are reading.

With pitch as a variable, it is vital that reading sessions are designed according to the level of individual competence expected. This will vary, but for a child to be able to follow and derive meaning from the text, language comprehension shouldn't drop too far below 80%. Think about the following:

- Independent reading: Pupils need opportunities to read texts that are pitched for success. If they are to be expected to read alone, a book ought to be almost completely decodable. For emergent readers, a phonically controlled book of just a few pages needs to be 100% decodable. For more competent readers, this would need to be no less than 95% (one word in 20) to avoid frustration kicking in.

- Guided reading: Throughout the week, there should be time for deliberate instruction of reading, perhaps with an adult working with a small group of pupils reading at a similar level. The pitch of the text needs to be slightly more challenging – 90–95% readable for instructional level – as the adult can scaffold the unknowns.

- Shared reading: This might be when the whole class reads a text as part of a writing lesson or during a whole-class reading session. The pitch could be 85–90% readable as there will be an element of co-reading (the teacher reads some, pupils read some).

- Modelled reading: When the teacher is reading to the class, the pitch can be as low as 80% as the teacher is doing all the legwork and will stop to explain and unpick every so often to keep comprehension levels strong.

Find opportunities for pupils to experience each of these scenarios across a week. The structure of reading lessons is up to the school and should be determined by the needs of the pupils, but if whole-class reading instruction is taking place, ensure there are opportunities for pupils to work with an adult to develop their reading skills based on their individual needs, rather than the average attainment of the whole class.

SLEUTHING

… when you have eliminated the impossible, whatever remains, however improbable, must be the truth.

Sherlock Holmes

Pupils need to experience a balanced reading diet across the week. As well as meeting a variety of different texts in different curriculum areas, they need different reading sessions for different aims. Before embarking on any reading activity with pupils, begin with some pre-teaching: a book introduction, a strategy check, a rehearsal of key words they are likely to meet or even re-reading a section of the text to warm up the 'reading muscles'. They are then ready to dig in and tackle the text with confidence.

A skilled reader approaches reading for comprehension in a similar fashion to a detective tracking for clues. They will scrutinise closely, ask pertinent questions, piece together all the evidence and make a final deduction.

An understanding of the language and subject matter of a text will allow a reader to know words and retrieve facts from the piece. But beyond this, there are several key competencies that are needed to build a stronger picture. Pupils must know what skills they need to draw upon and how they might use a particular skill to help piece their evidence together. How is an active reader getting all this information so effectively? What is their brain doing as they navigate a text?

INFERRING

In the dance of life, human beings must learn to understand not only what is directly presented to them, but also those things that are inferred; we might need to ascertain the implied meaning behind a painting, a gesture, a comment or a written word. Reading for meaning, like sleuthing, requires digging beyond what is literally there and trying to uncover what is hidden under the surface.

Jan ate a sandwich. He left the crumbs under the table. That night, the mice feasted.

When reading the above sentence, the reader must bring some background information to bear, to understand that sandwiches are made from bread and that little pieces of bread are known as crumbs. They must also infer that Jan ate at the table, and that some crumbs dropped underneath it as he did so. The reader must fill in the gaps to deduce this information (*elaborative inferencing*) as it is not explicitly mentioned.

The use of pronouns in the second sentence requires the reader to make what are known as *cohesive inferences* and conclude that the 'he' refers to Jan. Between the second and third sentences, the reader might make a *causal inference* – Jan left a mess and this will have repercussions. In the final sentence, they must presume that mice found the leftovers and infer from the connotations of the word *feasted* that they like eating bread and that there were plenty of crumbs.

Across a text, a reader will also need to make a series of *global inferences*. What is the overall message of the piece? Do the structure and themes imply meanings associated with other similar models? Does what I am now reading confirm or deny my previous assumptions? Inferencing, therefore, requires considerable verbal reasoning and takes up a lot of working memory.

Pupils need to be supported to explore the strategies the brain uses to make deductions and inferences. The following strategies might be a useful way in.

Visualising

Most writers try to paint a picture in your mind as you read their words. They want you to envisage what they envisaged as they wrote. If you are the sort of person who creates a definitive picture in your mind as you read, seeing the film of a work of fiction can be a disconcerting and sometimes disappointing experience: 'That's not how it should look!' But if you ask a group of children what they are picturing as they read, you'll notice that many of them don't realise that good comprehenders are typically seeing a movie in their minds as they read.

Through visualisation, a reader becomes more engaged with – and immersed in – the text. Picturing the scene enables the reader to understand how all the pieces of information connect, which helps them to remember the details and understand them. And, of course, they can monitor any incongruous information in the image, such as a doorway in the horse rather than the house!

Support pupils to develop visualisation skills in the following ways:

- **Before you begin reading**: Tell pupils to turn the TV on in their minds.
- **During reading**: Pause every so often to ask, 'What do you see when you close your eyes now?' or 'I imagined the character looking like this. What did you picture?'
- **After reading**: Ask them to draw a quick sketch of the scene and label it. They can then compare details with each other.

Summarising

Support pupils to solidify their global understanding of a text by inviting them to summarise it. Being able to successfully 'zip up' as they read will help pupils monitor for sense and retain key ideas. By condensing a passage into its essential points, they will also begin to recognise key themes.

Mix up your approach by asking them to:

- produce a six-box storyboard of the whole plot
- draw a diagram of a setting or character and label the key features
- write a synopsis of a paragraph in 20 words or less
- list the main ideas on the fingers of one hand
- choose five words that sum up the tone of a chapter

- create a story map or flow chart of key events
- take it in turns to retell the story: one pupil, one sentence (in six sentences if a group, or 30 sentences if the whole class).

Predicting

Young children begin very quickly to use their knowledge of the world around them to make predictions in stories. 'How might mum react when she sees this?' 'What might the dog do next?' The answers to questions such as these lie in our direct experiences.

With a burgeoning knowledge of the causes and effects typically seen in texts, hypotheses can then be built on common patterns in literature: 'I think they will get captured by the pirate and things will get tough for a while, but they will be rescued in the end' is a realistic supposition based on similar story arcs with a crisis before the 'happy ever after'.

- Explore the front cover and use clues in the title and images to guess the genre of the book and any themes. Read the first page and revise or confirm initial ideas.
- Encourage pupils to use the detail of the text to support their predictions. Make a grid using the headings 'Prediction' and 'Evidence' and ask pupils to suggest what might happen to various characters in a story.
- Use the language of probability between 'impossible' and 'definite' to help rein in wild suggestions. Where would they place their predictions? Highly unlikely because … Almost certain because …

Empathising

Empathy is a vital life skill and it supports readers to connect with their text-prediction skills. Teaching pupils to draw upon personal experience to imagine 'if I were in their shoes' is a way into understanding. Questions to build empathetic responses not only allow pupils to engage with characters but also further develop prediction, verbal reasoning and questioning skills:

- Have you ever had something like this happen to you?
- How might you feel if you were in his position?
- How might you feel if you were as lonely as Frieda?

- How would you react if you were told to leave your home?
- In what way does the extinction of these creatures impact you?

Pupils who struggle to empathise or see another's point of view can be supported through explicit modelling of empathy, exploration of emotions through play, as well as with 'social story' interventions.

Connecting and comparing

Good readers relate what they already know to the new information in the text. This helps them understand complex ideas more easily. When watching a *Mission Impossible* film, for example, you don't have to be a spy or to have jumped out of a plane to connect to emotions of fear and loathing or themes of good versus evil. Books work in the same way. Rather than getting frustrated when an examinable text presents a context that seems to favour children who have been camping or been on safari, we need to ensure that pupils have the skills to identify with any text. Build connections through questions like:

- Does this story remind you of anything you have read or seen?
- Do you know any other characters like this?
- What typically happens in this type of story pattern?
- How are these themes like the last text we read?

Questioning

Empower the pupils to ask questions and interrogate the text. Posing questions during reading should be natural; the active reader will be monitoring for understanding by making suppositions, answering and refining as they go. Children need to see that questions are not for after reading or purely the domain of the teacher. Support them to use tentative language as they formulate their hypotheses as this will help them feel safe enough to speculate without committing to a definite point of view:

- Could it be that …?
- Might he be …?
- I wonder if she …
- Maybe they will …
- Perhaps it's because …

The brain of a skilled reader works at lightning speed to synthesise the information from the print and process the language behind it. Life experience, literary knowledge, understanding of the nuances of language and reasoning skills enable readers to interrogate the text and derive meaning.

The Reading Framework (DfE, 2023a) reminds us that the skills of reading for comprehension cannot be taught in isolation. For example, knowledge of vocabulary helps us to analyse authorial choices and their impact; prediction using information within the text is a strand of inference. It is far more effective to explore a text holistically, drawing on a range of skills to piece together the evidence. Instead of asking a 'retrieval question' or an 'inference question', try asking pupils, 'What could you draw upon to answer that?' or 'What was your detective brain doing there?'

> # ASIDE
> ## ANSWERING
> A child. A book. A read. A chat. This is the way the mind grows. Not with a test but a tale.
>
> Michael Rosen
>
> At present, primary and middle schools must enter their Year 6 pupils (with few exceptions) for the national reading assessment tests. These focus on reading elements of the national curriculum and fall under eight domains for the purpose of analysis:
>
> | Content domain reference | |
> |---|---|
> | 2a | give/explain the meaning of words in context |
> | 2b | retrieve and record information/identify key details from fiction and non-fiction |
> | 2c | summarise main ideas from more than one paragraph |
> | 2d | make inferences from the text/explain and justify inferences with evidence from the text |
> | 2e | predict what might happen from details stated and implied |

Content domain reference	
2f	identify/explain how information/narrative content is related and contributes to meaning as a whole
2g	identify/explain how meaning is enhanced through choice of words and phrases
2h	make comparisons within the text

Source: English reading test framework 2016, National curriculum tests: Key stage 2. For test developers STA/15/7341/e, ISBN: 978-1-78315-826-3.

Improving comprehension takes practice and the development of strategies to make sense of different types of texts, from stories to news articles, poems to letters.

Where possible, avoid lists of test-style questions and keep the requirement for written answers low. As Michael Rosen attests, open-ended discussion goes further to develop children's comprehension than passively working through a comprehension exercise. Confident readers need relatively little guidance to navigate an exam paper, while endless SATs practice can fail to pay dividends when a pupil hasn't mastered the art of reading for meaning.

Likewise, try to keep questions and discussions open so that pupils avoid the 'guess the answer in the teacher's head' trap that can make them reluctant to join in. Once pupils are confident, volitional readers who enjoy discussing what they have read and have the skills to tackle whatever text comes their way, it's just a short step to convert that knowledge into effectively navigating a comprehension exam.

Try these activities for a holistic approach to comprehension:

- Carry out multiple reads of a text so that pupils build familiarity before being asked their opinion. A pre-read to build confidence and fill in background knowledge of vocabulary is invaluable for less confident readers or those with English as an additional language.
- Begin with straightforward reactions to the text: 'Did you enjoy reading it?' 'Would you recommend it?' 'Did you like the main character?' Children are

often surprised to be asked their feelings or opinions. They should feel safe enough to express dislike and to provide reasoning that doesn't match that of others.
- Give time for pupils to respond personally to the text. They might jot down questions, make predictions and highlight important parts as they read.
- Allow time for quiet, exploratory discussions before moving into groups or the whole class: 'Tell your partner one thing you know, one thing you think you know and one thing you would like to know.'
- Use Aidan Chambers' (1996) approach to invite deep thinking and go ever deeper without direct questioning: 'Tell me … Now tell me more … And what else …?'
- Older pupils can be exposed to the phrasing of exam questions during discussions: 'That's an interesting point. Which words and phrases gave you the impression that he was up to no good?'
- Encourage pupils to listen and respond to each other. They should learn how to offer an opinion, build on each other's contributions, ask for clarification and even disagree politely.

TENACITY

Our greatest weakness lies in giving up. The most certain way to succeed is always to try just one more time.

Thomas Edison

INCREASING STAMINA

In a recent Ofsted subject review for English, 'Telling the story' (2024), there was a suggestion that school leaders tend to perceive pupils' struggles with writing 'to be purely an issue with writing "resilience" and "stamina" – an issue with the child – rather than a curriculum weakness'. In truth, it is likely to be a bit of both; a child's resilience and stamina tend to be fragile, leading to dependence on adult support. The curriculum needs to be designed with that in mind.

So, if we accept that lack of reading and writing stamina can be a genuine problem for children, how can we build that endurance to support them in their journey towards automaticity in English skills?

Writing

It is widely acknowledged that writing was so much harder to teach remotely during lockdown. For many pupils returning to full-time school after periods of disruption, being asked to pick up a pen and perform sustained writing felt akin to being asked to undertake 20 laps of the local swimming pool.

In any given year, educators must acknowledge that September inevitably follows a period of non-writing, and the curriculum should factor that in. When a skill is embedded, strong and long practised, it is easier to keep going without tiring. It is also easier to pick up after an absence; the performer can build that stamina back quickly and independently.

With that in mind, there should be time to review learning from the previous year, to re-ignite knowledge, confidence and endurance. Activities involving sustained reading and writing need to be planned with care, taking into consideration the demands of the rest of the curriculum too.

Revisiting foundational skills, shoring up confidence in basic sentence structure and punctuation, and having the opportunity to re-establish expectations for punctuation, handwriting and spelling will all help to put learners in a positive space for moving forward for the rest of the year. This is where that well-designed curriculum comes in – opportunities to spiral back and consolidate learning so that pupils build automaticity in each skill.

Across the year, there should be a graduated approach to the quantity of writing expected. Brain tiredness aside, a writing arm that hasn't been performing the concentrated fine-motor movements associated with handwriting will struggle to write a story in the morning and complete a history report in the afternoon along with all the other incidental writing tasks in between. Terms that start with a poetry unit are a great way into a busy term of writing, not only in terms of limbering up language skills but also by reawakening the writing muscles. On the whole, a sprint through a poetry unit is easier on readiness for writing than a marathon of story writing.

If you have pupils in your class who start well but rarely have the 'oomph' to get to the end of a writing task, you will find that they end up with a book full of half-finished – or barely started – pieces of writing. Not only will it affect their self-esteem, but they won't develop any sense of creating satisfying endings. In KS2, this will begin impacting their ability to craft a cohesive text; pupils need to link sentences within and across paragraphs as well as take a reader on a journey through an entire text.

While, ultimately, the aim is for a pupil to write an entire piece, a good interim measure is to supply them with an example beginning and middle so they can experience writing a conclusion and learn the associated language skills and rounding-off techniques. With older pupils, provide the content of the piece in sectioned bullet points so that the pupil learns to flesh out and link ideas into cohesive paragraphs, rather than recording one undeveloped, unconnected idea at a time.

Consider group writing tasks where, after planning together, each pupil writes a section of a text and the group pieces everything together at the end. Allocate roles to members of the group so that pupils focus on the section(s) that will yield most benefit to them as individual learners. Pupils must edit as a group to make sure the piece hangs together as a collaborative, cohesive piece of writing.

Non-chronological reports, by their very nature, lend themselves particularly well to co-construction. If each pupil takes a section, a few magical things happen. First of all, the joint planning means that the pupil who might struggle with ideas is supported to build a direction of travel for their writing. The second is that once the sub-headings have been shared out, the amount of writing for each pupil is far less overwhelming than if they each had to write a complete piece.

During the writing stage, team spirit tends to kick in and, consequently, few children are inclined to let down their peers by failing to produce an outcome. Similarly, if they start to flail, one of the more confident writers will be on hand to give support. And the final advantage is that a pupil who may rarely get to present a completed piece of work can proudly claim joint authorship of the published project.

Reduce cognitive load

It stands to reason that because writing is a skill of many sub-skills, we need to build independence and stamina in each of these areas in order to increase output. In particular, we need to build pupils' transcriptional fluency – ensuring that handwriting and spelling skills are as automatic, fluid and accurate as possible – in order to allow space for pupils to think about composition and creativity.

If my computer becomes slow to respond, I tend to close some tabs or applications that are running in the background. In the same way, we can lessen the cognitive load for pupils during a task by removing some of the elements of writing and allowing them to build confidence and stamina in one focused area.

If it's quantity we are after, we could suspend spelling expectations and explain that if the pupil doesn't know how to spell a word, they should put a line underneath it and come back later. Handwriting expectations can also be dropped; pupils should write in a style that is comfortable to them, as long as it is legible.

Alternatively, the compositional element could be removed by setting the task around a familiar context or by providing the subject matter. In the example below, from a Year 1 child in autumn term, the complexity of the task has been reduced by inviting pupils to adapt the language patterns of the book they had been reading (Michael Rosen's *We're Going on a Bear Hunt*) in order that they might focus on accurate sentence structure and writing without adult support.

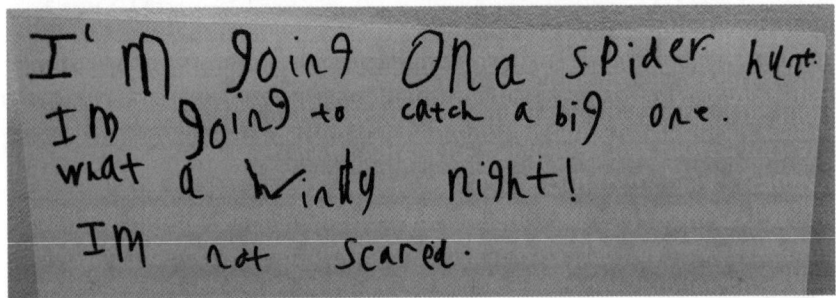

It might also be worth examining the success criteria and stripping the list back in any given writing session to keep new skills down to a minimum. If the objective is for a pupil to evidence conjunctions in their writing, we make that the focus, rather than also expecting half a dozen other recently acquired grammar skills to be included. We can reduce some of that mental stress of writing by sticking to just the core skill and gradually building up to a final piece that pulls everything together.

Build the pace

By KS2, lack of stamina becomes a problem: evidencing effective writing across a range of text types is rather tricky across only a few lines of writing. But just as pupils find it difficult to estimate how long to go until lunchtime, so do they struggle to understand how much writing they might achieve in a lesson. We can support them to regulate their time by structuring extended writing sessions to focus on pacing and incorporating focused breaks.

Try this strategy, for example: if you would like the class to write three paragraphs in 45 minutes, ensure first that the pupils have a clear plan of what they will write. Nothing eats into time more than trying to invent what to write next on the fly. Allow pupils time to read through the plan and then set them all off writing the introductory paragraph. After five minutes, tell them that they should be halfway through the paragraph and stop them promptly at the 10-minute mark.

Following a two-minute pit stop, in which pupils can read through and check what they have written so far, everyone needs to move on to the next paragraph. If the first isn't finished, they can leave a couple of lines, but they must start with everyone else. Repeat the steps from paragraph one: halfway warning, pit stop and move on.

By the end of the third paragraph, there should be time left for pupils to check this final section and then go back over the entire piece. In the remaining minutes, they can make revisions. Any pupils who need to can go back and add to incomplete paragraphs. They should all check that their writing hangs together as a complete piece.

As you repeat this exercise over time, pupils should be able to record more and more in the session. Do note, however, that when pupils are writing to time, handwriting expectations may need to take a bit of a backseat.

Build stamina in handwriting

Most of us will struggle to maintain beautiful handwriting over a sustained period, whether that be when writing feedback on the 30th book in the pile or taking notes for an hour. Children are no different.

You may notice a mismatch between the script a pupil can produce in a handwriting practice book and their writing in a piece of independent narrative. That's because when time and focus are given solely to handwriting, most pupils can give a concerted effort for the duration of that task. Conversely, when they are juggling multiple disciplines within compositional as well as transcriptional skills, something will have to give. And that's before we've even thought about the muscle strain caused by sustained control of a writing implement.

At times, we need to consider whether we want quality of handwriting or quantity of content: we may need to accept that we can't always have both at first. Gradual stamina building is needed.

Can the pupil give you one line of their 'gold-standard' (possibly joined) handwriting today before they drop back to a more relaxed script? What about two great lines tomorrow? Can we aim for a short paragraph next week? This technique is particularly useful when you have pupils who cannot sustain a joined script when writing at speed. This training method gives permission to write in a joined hand for a while then revert to print if they find that easier until they have developed the skill.

Even then, we need to consider when to expect 'publishing handwriting' and when to accept 'everyday handwriting'. If stamina continues to be an issue at that stage, could the pupil choose a short section of a story or written activity that they would like to edit and publish in a polished form?

In the example below, a Year 6 pupil is building their 'gold-standard handwriting' across the week as they write an extended composition based on *The Field Guide* (*The Spiderwick Chronicles,* Book 1) by Holly Black and Tony DiTerlizzi.

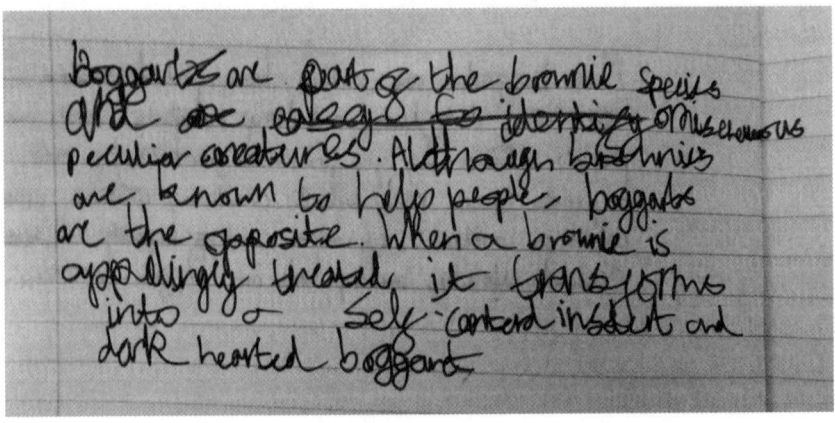

> These creatures are easy to identify, their skin is verdant and they're often humpbacked with unused minute wings. They often use ragged pieces of cloth for clothes for clothing and are often spotted carrying missing objects. Whatever they find that's either sharp, dangerous or shiny they will keep. For this reason, you should not leave important belongings unsupervised.

> Most boggarts are found in houses and mansions. They love living dark, dusty and damp habitats such as people's attics. If you find one in your home, try not to provoke this malevolent creature or leave precious belongings unattended. If taken care of boggarts will reward reward you by turning back into helpful brownies.

Through patience, persistence and by setting achievable goals, teachers can support pupils to build the stamina they need for making writing a sustainable and enjoyable practice. A well-considered curriculum incorporates strategies to develop endurance and confidence. We just need to remember – it's a marathon not a sprint.

> # ASIDE
> ## STAMINA FOR READING
> The same principles apply when considering stamina for reading. Compare a book-loving Year 6 pupil in September to a six-year-old child returning to school after a summer of no reading. It's not surprising that there is a drop back for pupils when their decoding skills are less secure; when that stamina is still in the making.
>
> As with writing, there are diverse yet complementary skills that the brain needs to use to make sense of a text. The energy a young reader expends as they try to pull these together is phenomenal. Consequently, novice readers tire easily and stamina building needs to be mapped into their reading training. In the same way as writing, fluency of skills plays a huge part in that stamina building: automaticity and accuracy of decoding, a natural pace and a prosodic quality all enable the reader to maintain focus and rhythm while building comprehension.
>
> The chapter on fluency delves into this in more detail, but try these ideas to build stamina too:
>
> - Gradually increase the number of sentences pupils are expected to read independently in a reading session.
> - As books progress through any scheme, the quantity on a page or number of words in the book increases. Try giving pupils a couple of easier books from time to time to allow them to develop stamina at an easier pitch.
> - Employ paired-reading and group-reading activities so that pupils can take it in turns to read a sentence, paragraph or page. They get to 'rest' in between turns but read more of the text overall.
> - In the same way, invite carers or reading volunteers to scaffold the learning to help pupils get through a book and stay motivated. If they are flagging as they read aloud, the adult can take over for a page or two to keep the reading going.

UNDERSERVED

Your curriculum should whisper – you belong.

Dr Dan Nicholls

According to recent statistics (Department for Statistics of England & Wales, 2022), 26.6% of the population of England and Wales do not identify as 'white British', 24% of the UK population has a disability (House of Commons Library, 2024) and around 22% of children in the UK are living in poverty (Department for Work and Pensions, 2024).

Despite making up a significant part of our school population, pupils represented in these statistics are disproportionately represented at the lower end of assessment data for reading and writing. If we accept that a child's ethnicity, socioeconomic background or learning needs do not automatically dictate their ability to read or write, then the only conclusion is that we are underserving huge numbers of children.

Who are the underserved pupils in your school and in what way are their experiences of the primary English curriculum perpetuating feelings of disenfranchisement? Putting your pedagogy and classroom organisation under the spotlight might reveal some practices that could be tweaked, or even radically overhauled, to better serve pupils who feel marginalised, undervalued or inadequately supported with their literacy skills.

PUPILS WITH SPECIAL EDUCATIONAL NEEDS AND DISABILITIES (SEND)

In January 2024, there were around 1.7 million school pupils in England with identified special educational needs (SEN), representing just over 18% of pupils. Less than 5% of pupils currently have an Education,

Health and Care plan, leaving around 13.6% of pupils who require SEN support in school but attract no additional funding (Department for Education, 2024b). These pupils should be everyone's business, but all too often the pressures on time and resources, combined perhaps with lack of specialised training, mean that provision is left to a classroom assistant or an overstretched SEN and disabilities coordinator. The result is that, in many cases, the pupils with the most need in schools are underserved.

The Education Endowment Foundation (EEF) guidance report 'Special educational needs in mainstream schools' (2021) suggests that the attainment gap between pupils with SEND and their peers is double that between pupils eligible for free school meals and their peers. Data from 2024 for pupils at the end of KS2 shows that only 21% of those with SEN attained the expected standard in reading, writing and maths.

Since the Covid-19 pandemic, there has been a renewed focus on narrowing the attainment gap for pupils with additional learning needs. Where schools are committed to developing effective support for these pupils, the starting point is evaluating current provision and adapting what is planned and done in the classroom. Primary English lessons are especially crucial; children need the means and tools to be able to read, write and communicate across the rest of the curriculum.

Well-designed, well-targeted and well-delivered interventions can work wonders to close gaps, but they need to be evaluated and monitored regularly. Ensure that pupils are working with adults who can offer that support effectively. All too often, the pupils with the greatest need are working with the people with the least training or experience.

If you have additional adult support, liaison between adults is vital to ensure a continuum of practice and a reinforcement of learning. Knowing which spelling patterns have been taught in an intervention means this learning could be woven into a class model. Knowing which vocabulary a pupil found challenging in a pre-read with the teaching assistant means the teacher could revisit those word definitions in the main lesson. Time taken to jointly discuss possible speaking frames for the lesson ahead is time well spent.

Careful consideration should also be given to what pupils will miss if they are withdrawn from the main teaching and learning. As well as potentially excluding pupils from lessons where they may experience enjoyment and success, interventions can widen the gap.

Where possible, interventions for reading should be in addition to – not instead of – the main lesson. The general principle is that pupils need more practice, not alternative practice. Recent advice in terms of SSP schemes is that the emphasis should be on supporting pupils to keep up with their phonics, rather than catch up.

Sometimes, adaptations to the main teaching are the most effective way of enabling pupils to access the learning. The EEF 'Five-a-day approach' (2024) suggests teachers embed the following five strategies into everyday practice:

- explicit instruction
- cognitive and metacognitive strategies
- scaffolding
- flexible grouping
- use of technology.

These are well within the wheelhouse of all teachers and could benefit any pupil with gaps in their learning, but the fourth strategy is one that seems to meet resistance. All too often, pupils with SEND are glued to a classroom assistant, perhaps with the same crew of lower-attaining pupils, lesson after lesson, regardless of content. If the remaining strategies are rigorously employed, then the fourth point will fall into place more readily.

Flexible grouping is a powerful tool for inclusion, as well as building independence. The SEND 'Code of practice' (DfE, 2015) advises: 'The purpose of identification is to work out what action the school needs to take, not to fit a pupil into a category.' Avoid making assumptions about what a child can or cannot do and design support according to pupils' specific learning needs (as well as learning preferences and strengths) in any lesson, rather than according to any label.

When planning support in English, try to consider all pupils who might benefit from a specific scaffold or group working. Targeted work on areas such as developing vocabulary, communication skills or handwriting might support numerous pupils with a need. On other occasions, a pupil may have a learning strength that means they could be challenged to work independently.

High-quality teaching for pupils with SEND is what good teaching for all pupils looks like and involves knowing your pupils well and understanding and adapting to their needs. A positive, supportive environment where all children can thrive will benefit all pupils, but especially those requiring additional learning support.

CHILDREN EXPERIENCING ECONOMIC DISADVANTAGE

Far too many pupils experiencing economic disadvantage leave primary education without having attained the national expected standard in English. In other words, they have not attained the standard that they could have expected to achieve if the playing field were level. As inclusion expert Daniel Sobel (2018) remarks: 'The attainment gap between disadvantaged pupils and their peers is one of the most insidious social injustices in the developed world.'

There is a notable crossover with economic disadvantage and SEN. The EEF notes that pupils with SEN are twice as likely as their peers to be in receipt of the Pupil Premium Grant (PPG; funding provided to UK schools to improve educational outcomes for disadvantaged pupils). Where there are learning gaps, tackle them swiftly to prevent them widening, using a range of strategies targeted to a pupil's need. Look out for any signs that pupils entering school are struggling in speech and language, phonemic awareness or vocabulary development as these gaps in foundational learning will cause barriers to new learning.

Step in to build reading mileage where home circumstances might mean parents or care givers cannot read with pupils outside of school. Make such children daily readers and ensure they have a range of audiences, including male role models, peers and the headteacher.

Avoid sweeping generalisations: there are lots of reasons why support for homework might not be forthcoming, but lack of care or interest should never be an assumption. Conversely, not all pupils from low-income households lack academic support; not all pupils in this category have gaps in learning. Check that all staff have high aspirations and that all pupils, regardless of background, are challenged and supported to reach – or exceed – age-related expectations in reading and writing.

The Pupil Premium Grant (PPG) is in place to ensure that no pupil gets left behind owing to poverty. Aside from the general considerations that might be put in place to address that, look at areas specific to literacy where lack of money might impact a child's experience, and you might make a difference.

Access to books is an obvious area of disparity. Lack of access to a library and low figures of book ownership among economically disadvantaged families are well recorded. Beyond using the PPG to purchase books for children, think creatively to build book ownership. Enlist the support of charities and book donations, hold book swaps and use commission from book fairs, for example.

Do the themes in books assume a shared knowledge of activities that pupils may not have experienced such as baking, trips to the zoo or riding a bike? If so, build connections with pupils' actual experiences and create new experiences in school that children can draw upon. Analyse writing units: do writing tasks make some pupils feel excluded? Adjust tasks so that they become more inclusive of all experiences.

Schools must safeguard the learning of all pupils by making certain than no one is underserved and everyone feels that they belong. Curriculum design is key. Is the curriculum structured to allow for the revisiting of skills? Does it allow pupils to see themselves reflected in the learning and to have a voice? If the curriculum feels logical, supportive and relevant to our most disenfranchised pupils, and inspires values that are upheld by all, then all pupils should hear loud and clear that they belong.

And finally, ensure school budget cuts don't impact on activities that benefit all but serve to build the cultural capital of economically disadvantaged pupils. These children have the most to gain from trips to the local theatre, zoo, seaside or museums. Ensure these pupils are actively encouraged to join after-school clubs that will build their sense of belonging as well as provide experiences that might inform their reading and enrich their writing.

When pupils have gaps in learning, or are at risk of falling behind, equity rather than equality is the key. Equality is dividing a loaf of bread equally between some hungry people. Equity is giving more bread to those who have not eaten in days, less to those who are not at risk of starvation. Rather than a mantra of 'all pupils should have an equal part of my time', remember that some children need you more than their peers to close the gap and level the playing field.

ASIDE
THE LANGUAGE OF INCLUSION

Language has always been organic, but it seems ever more so in our rapidly evolving society. Words have power: choosing the right terms when discussing people or themes is vital, especially when we are in classrooms with young people who are still forming a sense of their own identity and those who feel underserved by society.

It can feel tricky to navigate current acceptable language, particularly when referring to ethnicities, gender or disability, and this can cause anxiety about unwittingly causing offence. Ensuring that the school has an up-to-date language policy can help staff and pupils keep abreast of terms and develop more inclusive, non-discriminatory language across the school.

As well as verbal language, check that written language or any images in resources avoid stereotypes and are sensitively portrayed. While teachers can make judicious choices about the class novel or a history textbook, it's difficult to police every piece of literature on the bookshelf that a pupil might select.

The debate over whether we should ban specific authors or censor individual books will go on; there is a huge back catalogue of 'classic literature' to consider. Unfortunately, in an effort to increase diversity in their books, some modern authors have created clichéd tropes or used language that has moved on. The irony is, therefore, that the very books designed to redress the balance may not stand the test of time.

We should seek to make teachable moments when pupils stumble across discriminatory language or stereotypical scenarios. A discussion of why certain language is not considered appropriate and what they should do if they hear discriminatory terms will empower pupils to recognise and call out derogatory language or unconscious bias.

Representation goes beyond books – dictations, vocabulary definitions and discussions could all incorporate cultural references and visualise a wide range of identities. Examine your written models, for example. Do they perpetuate the traditional scenario of family life, or do they feature single parents, same-sex parents, stepfamilies and young care givers? Are all characters white, non-disabled people living in comfortable houses? We'll know we're getting it right when pupils feel empowered to tell their own stories and don't try to fit their writing to a mould that they believe is better valued by school or society.

Not only do opinions matter, but how children speak also matters. All too often pupils feel that their home language is not as highly regarded as English or that their accent, dialect or register is unwelcome in the classroom. This perception, whether based in reality or not, can silence pupils who do not feel confident to speak using 'standard English'. Encourage pupils to share their voice by sharing their life experiences and perspectives and telling people how they would like to be referred to.

VERSE

> You can find poetry in your everyday life, your memory, in what people say on the bus, in the news, or just what's in your heart.
>
> Carol Ann Duffy

In 2023, CLPE and Macmillan published the 'Poetry in primary schools' report. Their survey of almost 500 teachers across the country sought to explore the role of poetry in the primary curriculum. They discovered that while 80% believed 'poetry was a significant part of a literacy curriculum' and 88% thought that 'their children enjoyed engaging with poetry', only 38% of teachers felt confident enough to plan their own poetry units of work and 61% reported that they had never had any training on poetry.

Little wonder, then, that poetry is often the first casualty of the overloaded curriculum when time gets tight.

Nonetheless, it is generally acknowledged that poetry holds significant importance in primary education as a means of developing pupils' oral and written language, supporting their creativity and building empathy. Find the right poets and verse and you can move mountains in terms of children's learning. A well-planned curriculum acknowledges the value poetry brings to children's emotional and language development.

EMOTIONAL INTELLIGENCE

A fundamental superpower of poetry is that it allows pupils to understand, explore and express their feelings in a safe and structured way.

A sure-fire way in is through humour. Children love to laugh, and they love nonsense and vulgarity; some of the most successful modern writers are people who understand that: Michael Rosen, Julia Donaldson, Joshua Seigal, Neal Zetter. These writers created poems that demand to be read aloud and laughed over with others. And – just like jokes – comic verse is funniest when shared.

A writer who can provoke any reaction has successfully connected with their audience. Beyond laughter, poems can incite rage or draw tears, inspire sympathy and develop affinity. The famous war poets were not only processing what they saw and experienced but were aiming to connect to the hearts of their readers, to educate about their situation and to engender an empathy that just might change the future.

More recently, the Nicola Davies collection *Choose Love* seeks to offer an insight into the struggles and experiences of refugees and thereby evoke awareness and sensitivity. Reading poems about different experiences and perspectives helps children to identify with others by understanding their emotions and thoughts.

It can feel that now, more than ever before, we are simultaneously experiencing global connection and disconnect. Poetry can provide a way into the cultural experiences of others and a means of re-establishing love and hope.

LANGUAGE DEVELOPMENT

Poetry has a crucial place in language development as children begin to hear creative, rather than just functional, language. Early verse is accessible, fun, catchy and informal. Pre-school rhymes lead naturally to playground rhymes, which are organic, reflective of the culture and times, and often feel deliciously 'edgy' for young children. These are typically the gateway into more formal poetry studied within the classroom, but nevertheless provide good grounding in the language structures employed in literature.

Poems often use unconventional structures, exposing pupils to language play and alternative syntax. Consider Spike Milligan's titular line 'Down the stream the swans all glide', or the action rhyme 'Row, row, row your boat', which ends with the enigmatic but aurally satisfying line: 'Life is but a dream.' Poetic language encourages children to think creatively about sentence construction and grammar in a safe, 'anything goes' way. There are few wrong answers in poetry and that builds confidence.

Writing poetry allows pupils to experiment with language and express themselves creatively. The economical structure of many poems means limited use of conjunctions and extended clause structures, or complexities such as adding fronted adverbials or dialogue, so pupils can focus instead on their choice of words.

While there are many examples of lengthy, narrative verse, typically one associates the internal structure of lines of verse with succinctness. Poetry is an art form, like a painting, in which the artist seeks to evoke an emotion, an image, an idea and capture it like a fleeting moment. The economy of words is not a paucity, however; far from it.

Poetry is a genre in which every word has been chosen and positioned for maximum effect on the reader. At its best, there is not a single superfluous syllable. The precision of language means that children are often introduced to new words and phrases through poetry, and the format tends to make the language more accessible and more memorable. And perhaps, like a painting, when the meaning is not clear, it is left open to individual interpretation.

You can still enjoy a poem's rhythm and mood even when the vocabulary is beyond your current knowledge; maybe as some people enjoy songs in other languages. An extreme, but perfect, example of this is *Jabberwocky* by Lewis Carroll. For years, this poem was a staple in my drama club; I never met a child who didn't relish every nonsensical line. While the individual words are unfathomable, the sense of the poem is clear and children tend to act it out quite intuitively.

Poetry is often the first place children meet imagery and metaphor. Each word in a poem needs to earn its place by painting a vivid picture. For example, in the uncluttered line structure of *The Sound Collector* by Roger McGough, children should readily hear the onomatopoeia jump out. In *The Sea* by James Reeves, there is a first line in which the only words are the metaphor 'The sea is a hungry dog', and every subsequent line further exemplifies that anthropomorphism. It is relatively easy for children to spot, and understand, the imagery.

A well-written poem creates vivid images in our minds and, in turn, supports pupils to apply imagery in their own writing. And a well-written poem demands to be shared.

PERFORMANCE

The current primary English curriculum asks that pupils can learn by heart and recite poetry. It is good to see that poetry has its rightful place in the new curriculum and that children will be expected to learn poems. This shouldn't be by rote and drill for the sake of a curriculum directive, but rather through the repeated, joyful readings that cause a poem to stick to your soul, like toffee to your tooth.

Following on from the perfect simplicity of nursery rhymes and counting rhymes, poems such as Christina Rossetti's *Mix a Pancake* ('Mix a pancake, Stir a pancake, Pop it in the pan ...') or Allan Ahlberg's *Please Mrs Butler* ('Please Mrs Butler, this boy Derek Drew ...') have a rhythm and life of their own, with rhyme schemes so perfect that you don't so much learn the poems as have them attach themselves to you. Did you consciously learn *The Owl and the Pussy-Cat* off by heart or has it simply lodged in your memory like the lyrics of a popular song?

If you've ever felt the pride of watching that oh-so-very-shy pupil perform a poem in a class assembly or judged a children's poetry competition, you'll agree that, somehow, reciting verse in front of others can boost pupils' confidence and help them become more comfortable with public speaking. And speaking out loud is a vital skill. Joseph Coelho, former Children's Laureate, once wrote: 'Something special happens when you read poems aloud, you start to feel yourself get a little braver, a little more confident.'

Like songs, there is perhaps a certain predictability of language that arises in poetry. This potentially makes it easier to learn by heart than prose and gives a pupil confidence to recite it aloud, in front of others, in a way that they may not normally do. Again, like singing, poetry can be a social experience. Poems are usually written with performance in mind: whether as a group recitation, dramatisation or even just an opportunity for a whole class to join in with a refrain. These sorts of experiences are essential in helping children develop skills of teamwork, listening and communication.

Young children love books with repetitive refrains when they are encouraged to join in. They will joyfully supply the final word in lines of stories told in rhyme. And because, as Gloria Estefan once sang, 'the rhythm is going to get you', children across the world have – for over 30 years – chanted the cadenced lines of Rosen's *We're Going on a Bear Hunt*. Hearing poetry – including stories told in verse – being read aloud, read with prosody and performed is a necessary step to enable pupils to internalise vocabulary and language structures that can then be used in their own spoken and written language.

Poems are also a great way of building reading fluency because, like a favourite song or picture book, they demand to be read again and again. Those repeated re-reads support internalisation and, of course, build towards a confident performance. And, like most songs and picture books, they often come in a brief, easily repeatable package.

CURRICULUM

Incorporating poetry into the primary school curriculum enriches children's educational experience, helping them grow academically, emotionally and socially. The creative and linguistic freedom it brings can engage and enchant even the most reluctant readers and writers. But choosing the poems, and where they fit, can be a tricky business. A poetry spine is increasingly being viewed as a 'must-have' in schools, but where to begin?

- Start from a place of love. What sorts of poems do you want pupils to experience in your curriculum?
- Plot out poets that children should read in the same way as you would other authors, including the best historic and current writers.
- Choose poems for their merit rather than because they happen to fit a topic like 'the Romans', for example.
- Consider representation and weave equality, diversity and inclusion into your book spine.
- Plan for progression in form as well as difficulty of language: list poems, calligrams and acrostics before narrative poetry and poems with extensive use of metaphorical language.

WRITING

There is, perhaps, a freedom in poetry that isn't always to be found in other forms of writing. As well as the actual words, there is a rhythm to be enjoyed; perhaps also a visual approach such as concrete poetry, acrostics and even the pleasing sight of repeated or onomatopoeic words.

Perhaps because it is seen to have less value than other written forms, poetry often gets left to the end of a busy term, where it can end up being rushed, curtailed or even abandoned altogether. It's the poor understudy in the curriculum, whereas it really ought to take centre stage.

If we recognise the value verse brings to pupils' language, moving a poetry unit to the beginning of a term can give you a vocabulary-rich start to inspire further writing. Not only will pupils enjoy the opportunity to explore new vocabulary as they craft their own poetry, they can explore and use words, phrases, metaphors and other literary structures.

The first teaching resource I ever bought for poetry was the (sadly now out-of-print) classic *Does it have to Rhyme?* because, of course, that's the question on every child's lips when they are told they will write a poem. When they *are* expected to rhyme, they can get tied in knots trying to force the words into place. The most liberating thing is to have an 'anything goes' approach at first and then look at tightening format or adding requirements for rhyme once children have understood the concept of word play. Young pupils can begin to experiment with rhyming by using nonsense poetry such as Spike Milligan's classic, *On the Ning Nang Nong*:

> On the Ning Nang Nong
> Where the cows go Bong!

That freedom extends to an ability to veer from formal or standard English, and many poets even employ regional dialect to express their ideas. Generations of readers have been captivated by vernacular writers like Geoffrey Chaucer, Robert Burns, Benjamin Zephaniah and Liz Berry. How better for pupils to begin writing about things that matter to them than by using their authentic voice? And with examples as rich as Valerie Bloom's *Granny Is* or Matt Goodfellow's *The Final Year*, children are spoiled for choice when it comes to inspiration.

VERSE

The key to writing poetry with children is to have fun: be liberated in your approach and the children will yield writing that they love. And no, it doesn't have to rhyme ...

ASIDE

It is worth checking whether the younger pupils know any classic nursery rhymes. In recent years, more and more children are arriving at school with no idea that Humpty fell off a wall, or that Little Bo Peep has lost her sheep. Nursery rhymes are an important step in phonological awareness. They are usually short and memorable, and generally employ a simple rhyme pattern, repetition and song-like rhythm – all of which support language development. They are designed to be heard, repeated and shared.

The internalising of these ditties focuses not on an understanding of their exact meaning but on phonemic knowledge, specifically onset and rime (i.e. the initial phoneme and the string of letters that follow). Hearing and memorising pairs of words like *saw/daw, Jill/hill, peep/sheep* sets children up to be able to distinguish between similar sounds, anticipate missing words and create strings of rhymes. This language play is crucial as it paves the way for meeting these sounds in early reading.

Traditional rhymes also have cultural importance. They may pertain to significant periods in history, people and places, such as *Ring-a-Ring o' Roses, London Bridge Is Falling Down* or *The Grand Old Duke of York*. Each language will have its own traditional rhymes and it is worth encouraging parents and carers to pass these on. Some overlap and some are unique to a specific heritage. Either way, hearing rhymes in a home language helps establish and maintain bonds to cultural heritage while supporting children to notice how words bounce along together in harmony.

WORDSMITHS

But words are things, and a small drop of ink,
Falling like dew, upon a thought, produces
That which makes thousands, perhaps millions, think.

Lord Byron

A rich vocabulary is a fundamental building block to all communication. It is integral to reading, writing and spoken language and critical to a pupil's success in all areas of the curriculum.

In recognition of the key role of vocabulary in academic achievement across the phases of education, most schools have now built in an element of vocabulary instruction. However, the rate at which children accrue new language doesn't always match the urgency of the disadvantage some pupils have in this area. Whether this be the '30-million-word gap' cited 30 years ago by Hart and Risley (1995), or a more conservative figure, the scale of the problem is undeniable.

Various educationalists have described the consequence of limited accessible vocabulary as 'the Matthew Effect' from the biblical reference to the propensity for 'the rich to get richer while the poor get poorer'. The more words a child has, the more new words they can unlock to create shades of meaning. A pupil with a limited word palette will struggle to make connections with existing words in their vocabulary and, without support, they will remain in lexical poverty.

Many of our young children arrive in school with a limited lexicon, which inevitably impacts communication skills as well as early reading development. True, children will naturally build language as they interact with the world around them and absorb new experiences. However, for most, this won't be enough. We need to give pupils robust opportunities to acquire vocabulary through activities that help them play with words: to explore, classify, categorise, compare, contrast, detect patterns and construct meaning.

To have impact, vocabulary instruction must be carefully planned. There should be a deliberate and logical rationale behind the inclusion of words and the activities used to introduce them. Children should not bump into new words or opportunities by chance.

The first step to rigour is to ensure a planned, consistent and school-wide approach to vocabulary acquisition. A survey of over 800 schools carried out by the Oxford University Press (2023) found that, despite it being a priority area in 90% of schools, only 52% of them had a vocabulary policy or school-wide strategy in place. Only 30% of schools used a specific vocabulary-building programme, and of those who did have something in place, only a third of the teaching staff found it to be beneficial.

A design for vocabulary instruction doesn't need to be a detailed list of all possible words that pupils need to be taught, but rather a roadmap of the how, when and the categories of what will be introduced. Opportunities for language development need to be woven into all corners of the curriculum and hooked onto concepts that will thread through the learning journey. All staff need to be aware of the route as well as the stops along the way. Above all, there needs to be a culture of rigour, vigour and language curiosity to ensure a whole-school approach.

The principle of tiers of vocabulary was introduced to us through the research of Beck, McKeown and Kucan (2013). They conceptualised the idea that words could be categorised by frequency and difficulty, thus offering a place to focus on vocabulary instruction. Broadly speaking, this could be represented like so:

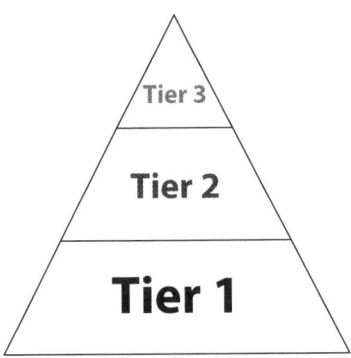

Tiers of vocabulary.

Tier 1 is the everyday language that pupils will assimilate through daily interactions; by and large, this will not need to be explicitly taught. By contrast, Tier 3 words need to be planned for and taught as the need arises so that pupils can access the concepts being shared. They should be mapped systematically across curriculum areas (perhaps included in knowledge organisers).

Tier 2 words are where we put our energy. These are the words that provide nuance to our language and might have multiple different meanings according to context. As long as pupils have a concept of these words and the Tier 1 language upon which to build, this layer provides a rich seam for language development, especially during the course of reading.

SUBTLETIES OF THE ENGLISH LANGUAGE

Because English is such a magpie of a language, we often end up with multiple words to describe the same thing. But there are few, if any, absolute synonyms: each variation of a word has a subtly different meaning. Think about the very Britishness of having an array of words to depict the capriciousness of our weather, including several just for the different types of precipitation!

This allows for such precision in our communication. Children have the power to convey a very particular picture to their audience if only they know about those nuances. A flick through the thesaurus doesn't always yield the best results: at best, they might find an alternative word without understanding the shades of meaning (e.g. *overjoyed* and *cheerful* are both synonyms of *happy*, but they sit at opposite ends of a happiness scale). The worst-case scenario is they pop in a word that doesn't suit every context. You might have an antique chair and an elderly grandmother, but you couldn't transpose those adjectives.

Support understanding of the subtleties of synonyms in the following ways:

- Ask your class: 'How shall we walk to assembly today? Let's march/trudge/walk/amble/hike/stroll/stride.'
- Build a collection across a week. For example, each group takes a colour and contributes to a visual thesaurus on the working wall – such as, red: ruby, poppy, blood; blue: navy, sky, duck egg – by bringing in a picture and adding it to their section.

As pupils assimilate new words and enjoy the sophistication of using alternatives to 'Tier 1 words', they can be prone to hyperbole. They might tell you at lunchtime that they are 'starving', when they had a snack an hour before, or that they're 'petrified' when they are just a little nervous. Design activities that support gradations of words by giving them collections of similar words that they then attempt to place on a scale from one extreme to another; for example:

- Place words pertaining to temperature on a thermometer ranging from freezing to boiling.
- Create a scale of happy to sad by labelling emoticons and putting them in order from least to most happy.

Children can resort to bland, catch-all terms when they don't know enough precise nouns to name subjects within a category. For example, they might write about a character living in a 'house' when 'cottage' or 'mansion' might have given the reader a clearer picture of the nature of the abode. Alternatively, they might overemploy adjectives to layer in some precision where a specific, proper noun might have done the trick. If you have pupils with a tendency to write phrases such as 'a big, black, snarling dog' when 'Rottweiler' could have been substituted, try this activity as a morning starter in teams: each group has 5 minutes to come up with as many precise nouns as possible for your given category (e.g. dwellings/vehicles/insects).

READING

Vocabulary knowledge is key to reading comprehension. Centre tuition on fostering an enjoyment of language and a thirst for exploration. Activities like this work well:

> Words cost £1 and you are given £10.
> Which words or phrases might you 'buy' from this piece of text?
> Why have you chosen them?

Ensure you teach and model strategies that will enable pupils to uncover word meanings independently, such as:

- Can you find the root word and build meaning from there by adding each affix: un<u>seat</u>ed, dis<u>appear</u>ing?
- Link to a word you know, for example: 'The apple <u>crumble</u> was delicious and they soon emptied their bowls.'
- Substitute a word with one in the same grammatical class and see if it makes sense: 'The candle <u>was snuffed</u> out.'

SPELLING

Spelling and vocabulary are inextricably linked. The expectation is that pupils will employ the spellings they are learning within their independent writing, but this is impossible if a child isn't sure how to use a given word in context. Effective spelling lessons explore the link between vocabulary, reading and writing and build strong connections. The added benefit is that clear mapping of the spelling curriculum gives each teacher a quick reminder of the vocabulary the pupils will have met in previous years.

Rather than unlocking words individually, expand pupils' vocabulary schema through use of morphology and word families. Considering the meanings of affixes can help pupils to attempt definitions of unfamiliar words using the same affix. For example, if we know that un- denotes an opposite state of being and we know the word *undo*, we can work out the meaning of *unhealthy* or *undiscovered*.

ORACY

Children are like sponges when it comes to assimilation of language. But in order to make new words stick, they need to encounter them in different contexts and make mental notes of their appropriate usage. The more they read and hear the same word, the faster they can begin to confirm or adjust their understanding. When confident enough, they can move the word from their receptive to productive vocabulary and try it out in their own speech or writing. As linguist Professor David Crystal once said: 'Vocabulary is a matter of word-building as well as word-using.'

Dialogic teaching can provide that bridge between receptive and productive vocabulary. You can expedite the process by grasping every moment to slot in a new word or revisit a recently used word. Scaffolding new vocabulary experiences by linking new words to existing knowledge provides a built-in definition. For example:

'I'm so thirsty. In fact, I'm parched. Have you ever felt parched?'

'Would you like to accompany me, to come with me? Who normally accompanies you on the way to school?'

Provide a verbal sentence frame that includes the target word for them to use in response.

Build spoken language confidence, including the pronunciation of words, through quick-fire vocabulary games. For example, a game of word tennis can be squeezed in at any time of day. Bounce words with similar meanings between each other in a word rally. The first person to drop the ball by running out of suggestions, or who gives a word that isn't right, loses.

Grammar games

Build pupils' grammatical knowledge by providing frames that allow them to construct sentences using sets of words in the same class:

Creative conjunctions:

Challenge the pupils to link three nouns in a sentence and change the meaning, e.g. *granny, knitting, Marmite.*

- Granny enjoys knitting <u>while</u> eating Marmite.
- Granny likes knitting <u>although</u> she isn't keen on Marmite.
- Granny finished her knitting <u>before</u> eating Marmite.

Active adverbs:

Mime coming into the room 'in the manner of the verb', e.g. energetically/quietly/joyfully/stealthily/angrily, and allow the pupils to guess the adverb.

Broaden pupils' vocabulary at every point of the day and err on the side of overstuffing rather than underdelivering. Word of the week is simply not enough. If we want to close the vocabulary gap and enrich pupils' language experiences, we need to zealously introduce and revisit word after word at every turn.

Try to follow a systematic pathway that allows for reinforcement and consolidation rather than randomly throwing dozens of words at pupils without context or repetition. A word met in a story could be explained in the context of the text, then used in a verbal exchange later in the day and incorporated into modelled writing opportunities during the week. Can the pupils be encouraged to apply that word in their own speaking and writing?

Above all, instil a culture of fun around word exploration. Encourage them to hunt and collect, build and dissect. In short, create a classroom of logophiles.

ASIDE

Pupils who have English as an additional language are often referred to in sympathetic tones. Advice seems to focus on the deficit model of the specific problems they might experience around conjugation of verbs or muddling of pronouns.

It can be hard to cater for children arriving in school with little or no English and limited resources to support them. But generally, children's resilience and curiosity makes for accelerated progress when they are immersed in the language through school.

Pupils with English as an additional language generally have a superpower: the ability to code-switch and build a rich bilingual — or even multi-lingual — vocabulary. If they are in the early stages of English acquisition, assist word building through dual-coded word mats, using plenty of actions to facilitate spoken exchanges. You could even use AI to generate translations.

Above all, ensure pupils are praised for their ability to communicate in two languages and show them that the skill is valued. At times, children (and their carers) can feel the need to bury their first language in preference for English. Dual-language books are one resource all bilingual children should have access to — even if they cannot read. Sharing these books at home allows them to continue to build rich vocabulary in their home language and use it to unlock the new language.

XYLOPHONE

English has been this vacuum cleaner of a language, because of its history meeting up with the Romans and then the Danes, the Vikings and then the French and then the Renaissance with all the Latin and Greek and Hebrew in the background.

David Crystal

X, as any self-respecting ABC book will assert, is for *xylophone*. Not for *exit* or *excuse*, although it does make an appearance in these words. *Xi* (Ξ pronounced 'ksai' to rhyme with *sky*) is the 14th letter of the Ancient Greek alphabet via Latin. Unsurprisingly, the word *xylophone* is also from Ancient Greece.

The letter 'x' is rarely found at the beginning of words in the English language and so generations of young children have been subjected to wondering what on earth a xylophone might be, and why it isn't making an appearance two pages further along in their alphabet book.

Frustratingly for some, 'z' is definitely not for *xylophone*; neither does it appear in *loser* or *cheese*. Pronunciation is no guide to spelling in a language that has been assembled over millennia using a range of different phonics systems. Rather than frustration, I find the complexities of the English spelling system intriguing and absorbing. Why is the number *two* written with a 'w'? Why do we pronounce the words *paid* and *said* differently?

The chequered history of this country leaves its legacy in our rich language, although the wealth it bequeaths can be the root of the spelling difficulties that some children experience.

The most frequently used words in the English language are typically those that refer to everyday objects, activities or emotions and these have always been part of our vocabulary; imported words are generally synonyms or words that add an extra layer to our basic communication. Of the most common 100 words used in the English language, all of them have Anglo-Saxon origins.

Unfortunately, pronunciation changes more rapidly than spelling, so the encryption of many Old English words often corresponds to articulation long since disappeared. The chaos of the *ough* letter string can be attributed to that process. Clues can sometimes be found in other, similarly spelled, words. If you think back to my earlier mention of *paid* and *said*, we can spot the same tense changes in spelling of *pay* to *paid* and *say* to *said* and begin to guess how *said* may have been pronounced in ages past.

The earliest spellings were the result of individuals attempting to record words to match the sounds, but regional variations in pronunciation were already in play. The invention of the printing press in the 15th century helped to standardise spelling, as did the first modern dictionary, published by Samuel Johnson in 1755. But by then, words from Latin, Greek and French were also locked into the language.

EXPLORE ETYMOLOGY

Let's go back to the title of this chapter. X is indeed for *xylophone*, but what does this intriguing word mean? Each syllable is a Greek root word: *xylo* meaning 'of wood' and *phone* meaning 'voice' or 'sound'. Physical exploration of the object will confirm that a xylophone is a musical instrument made of wood, each bar giving a different note or sound.

Pedants of language or music will note that the image seen in books is often of a colourful instrument, made of metal. Played in the same way, the two are often seen as interchangeable. However, the metal variant is, in fact, a glockenspiel rather than a xylophone. The etymology of this word is Germanic: *glocken* are 'bells' and *spiel* means 'play', so here we have a 'bell play' rather than the 'voice of wood'. In the words of the eponymous gladiator: 'Are you not entertained?'

Etymology – the study of the origins of words and their changing meanings and spellings over time – is one of the pillars of spelling, along with phonology and morphology. But can its yield ever be more than a mildly entertaining party piece or a 'fun' spelling investigation for children?

The good news is that pupils are often fascinated by the stories behind seemingly irregular spellings. You can use this engagement to support them to remember the spellings of trickier words.

The peculiar spelling of *two*

While its homophone *to* has the alternative variant of the *oo* phoneme (/uː/) spelled with one 'o', there is seemingly no logic to this word having a silent 'w' in the middle. Not until you explore the history of this word, that is. From the Old English words *twa* and *twegen*, representing the number that is 'one more than one', this number shares roots with other European languages including *dwa* in Polish, *två* in Swedish and *zwei* in German. The word *twain* has still just about survived in English, but we no longer hear the *w* sound that used to be pronounced in *two*. However, when we consider other words that are analogous (such as *twelve*, *twenty*, *twin*, *twice* and *between*), we can make an exciting comparison that may help to secure the spelling of this word.

Teaching other words with 'silent' letters

When teaching words with 'silent' letters, consolidate learning and build vocabulary by inviting pupils to explore the etymology behind the words. Almost certainly, the 'silent' part was once pronounced. In fact, artificial articulation can help to remind us of the silent part when spelling, for example, pronouncing 'island' as 'is-land'.

Year 2 and Year 3 pupils could investigate words beginning with 'kn' in this way:

> The 'kn' spelling, pronounced 'n' (/n/), is found in some very old words like 'knee' and 'know', and long ago the 'k' was sounded, so the words would have been pronounced 'k-nit' and 'k-now'. How many of these old English words can you find and can you discover their meaning? Have fun pronouncing them the old way and use this strategy to remember to add the 'kn' when you spell the word.

In some cases, you can provide linked words where the letter is heard to build helpful associations. Year 5 and Year 6 could explore patterns like this, for example:

> crumb > crumble
>
> limb > limber
>
> climb > clamber
>
> bomb > bombastic
>
> Invite pupils to investigate the meaning of the second word if they don't already know.

This metacognitive approach – understanding how and why words are spelled, along with the strategies that might help build and check a spelling – gives pupils tools for independence in writing. Ultimately, pupils need to build a broad knowledge of the orthographic system rather than relying on an adult or dictionary to supply or correct spellings.

BUILD SCHEMATA

These sorts of activities help to build a spelling schema in a pupil's mind; something to forge connections and hang on to. Pupils can't be expected to learn thousands of words in isolation; that way lies failure for all but those with an infinite photographic memory. Successful spellers may well be those with a good memory combined with skills of visualising. But they are undoubtedly behaving as squirrels: seeing a word and collecting it, storing it away in the correct larder with all the other similar words.

Support pupils to work on the deductive principle of 'If you know x, what else do you know?' to create ever-greater linked files of knowledge.

Many of the common exception words can be dealt with in this way. For example, pupils could compare how *pay > paid*, *lay > laid* and *say > said* all fit the same spelling pattern, even though the pronunciation has changed over time.

VOCABULARY DEVELOPMENT

Exploring the history of words also helps to uncover meaning, and that vocabulary knowledge allows us to build even more words, all of which link together in the relevant part of the word schema.

The web of spellings connects us to other languages and is useful for pupils' development of English as well as other tongues.

> For example, present pupils with the French word *mort*, meaning 'death' (from the Latin). Not only can they connect to that everyday French term, but they can use that knowledge to unlock the spelling and meaning of words like *mortal, immortality, mortuary* and even *mortified*.
>
> By contrast, the French word *habiter*, meaning 'to live' (also from Latin), gives us words like *habitat, uninhabited, habitation* and *habitable*.

The key to vocabulary development is the ability to unlock words from words; to use existing knowledge to fuel new learning. Understanding the meaning behind words gives pupils the confidence to use them in their writing. Usage in context reinforces knowledge of spelling and consolidates pupils' productive vocabulary. As with all aspects of literacy, the spellings of words and their meaning are inextricably linked.

HAVE FUN WITH WORDS

Above all else, it is important that children learn to enjoy words and spelling; to see the process as a fun code to crack rather than a battle to fight. To explore, experiment and test rather than be constantly tested. Etymology is the perfect basis for that word investigation.

In the words of David Crystal (2013), 'The story of the English writing system is so intriguing, and the histories behind individual words so fascinating, that anyone who dares to treat spelling as an adventure will find the journey rewarding.'

ASIDE

MORPHOLOGY

In KS1, pupils learn how to use an increasingly sophisticated range of suffixes to manipulate words and form word families using the base morpheme or root words. This enables them to change tense, form plurals and create comparative words. In Years 3 and 4, pupils are introduced to an array of prefixes beyond un-, which they are taught to use in Year 1.

In Year 2, pupils are taught that, at times, the root word needs to be altered slightly before adding the affix. Word play in this area is crucial as the rules are tricky to embed for some pupils. Revisit the rules again and again and across the year groups with ever-increasing pitch, for example, the removal of 'e' before the suffix -ing in *baking, creating, communicating, accommodating*.

Combined with etymology, this is a golden opportunity to exponentially expand pupils' spelling and reading power. As long as we supply meaning to the affixes as we go, pupils can use the individual morphemes at their fingertips like Lego bricks to construct spellings and deconstruct meanings. (See Section Two for some activities to try.)

YACHT

The English language is full of words that are just waiting to be misspelled, and the world is full of sticklers, ready to pounce.

Mary Norris

The spelling programme of study in the most recent national curriculum (DfE, 2013a) has informed spelling teaching in primary schools for over a decade now and contains over 100 different spelling objectives for children to master. Pupils must meet the spelling requirements listed in the Assessment Framework to be judged as working at an age-related standard at the end of each key stage.

Despite a decade of greater focus on phonics and spelling in schools, some pupils still struggle to meet the expected standard in writing because of gaps in their spelling knowledge. Ostensibly, the sticking point is retention and application of their current-year-group expectations. However, upon digging deeper, we find that many pupils do not have the firm foundations of spelling content from previous year groups on which to build.

If etymology is the 'why' behind spelling, then phonics is the 'what' and the 'how'. It is the foundation of all decoding and encoding that pupils learn at primary school. But with approximately 40 phonemes (speech sounds) versus 250 possible grapheme correspondences in the English language, it is an involved process to master all the possible variations.

To many educators charged with its delivery, the English spelling system may seem similarly hostile and unpredictable – and consequently difficult to teach. The word *yacht*, for example, doesn't fit any phonics taught and is a unique oddity of spelling. But is our spelling system as capricious as it appears? A study by Hanna et al. (1966) concluded that only 4% of commonly used words have spellings that cannot be predicted by their pronunciation.

While the expectation within a phonics scheme is that pupils simultaneously encode as they decode, there is invariably a mismatch between these two skills in young children; spelling ability tends to lag. We may hope that from the end of Reception onwards, pupils will use their emerging knowledge of phonics to spell any word of their choosing in a phonetically plausible way, but we should acknowledge that some children take longer to meet that expectation.

There also is a bias towards practising decoding for phonics over encoding, likely due to the time pressure to get pupils ready for the phonics screening check, which is, of course, a reading check and not a spelling check!

REVIEW LEARNING

Even without the lag factor of encoding, the sheer volume of spelling objectives in the KS1 curriculum necessitates a constant reviewing of even the earliest of phonics teaching as we progress.

In Year 3, this revision might begin with the long vowel phonemes from KS1. As they move into KS2, pupils are often selecting the correct phoneme but are still representing it with the wrong grapheme. For instance, they might spell the word late as 'layt' or 'lait'. This is phonetically plausible but not orthographically correct. Using the 'best bet' approach can help with this sort of difficulty. We could tell pupils that -ay is the best bet for the long *a* at the end of a word, but rarely in the middle; and that while 'ai' is a good option for the medial sound, the split a_e is often found where the final sound in the word is a *t*. This is knowledge that they may well have been taught but not retained.

Once pupils have grasped the principle of building root words from the constituent sounds using their phonetic knowledge, they need to be introduced gradually to the conventions of morphology – adding affixes to create families of words with the same root but having variations of meaning. The learning starts off simply, by adding suffixes such as -s, -ing and -ed that do not affect the root word. Gradually, pupils learn how to manipulate words by removing, doubling or substituting letters before adding affixes.

CLOSING LEARNING GAPS

With so much content being covered in KS1, it is little wonder that some pupils struggle with retention. The very first statement in each national curriculum spelling appendix, which clearly states that 'children should revise work done in previous years', should be emphasised more emphatically.

At the start of the Year 3/4 programme of study, in relation to revision of work from Years 1 and 2, it advises: 'Pay special attention to the rules for adding suffixes.' If you have a pupil in Year 6 who is still spelling *hopeful* with a double 'l' or *families* with a 'y', then the chances are that they have forgotten all about the Year 2 programme of study from four years ago. For some, the Year 2 programme of study may have eluded them altogether. Many of the suffixes, such as -ment, -less and -ness, are requirements for pupils working at the greater depth standard, so it's likely that some pupils were working on earlier spelling priorities or trying to secure early phonics at the time and have never been taught these conventions.

If we acknowledge that it is unreasonable to expect pupils to remember spelling patterns, rules or conventions from previous weeks, terms or years, then the principle of reviewing prior learning becomes an obvious necessity. Once we have embedded this into spelling instruction, we can both assess pupils' understanding and support them to establish connections in their long-term memory.

A systematic shoring up of the foundations of spelling knowledge, aided by strategies to secure retention, will help pupils with gaps in their spelling. The first step is the identification of the gaps to enable tracking back to prior learning.

It's important to pick the correct battles with that revision. Trusted primary practice revisits higher-stakes learning, such as spelling patterns and words that appear most often in the English language and are commonly misspelled. It's pointless teaching a pupil to spell *committee* correctly if you see *untill* appearing in their independent writing over and over.

COMMON EXCEPTION WORDS

While the route to successful reading and spelling acquisition lies in a systematic phonics approach, we don't get too far before we bump into that 4% of words that pupils need to use but that do not fit into the correspondences they have yet learned. And, unfortunately, those words represent the most frequently used vocabulary in the English language.

The words *no, go* and *so* are not accessible when at first you only know the 'o' grapheme making an *o* (ɒ) phoneme as in *hot* and *dog*. Some schemes call such words 'tricky' words, others 'red words'; the national curriculum refers to them as 'common exception words'.

These irregular spellings are taught alongside more readily decodable words and added gradually to keep cognitive load manageable for young children. By the time pupils leave Year 1, they should have been taught to read and spell the first 100 highest-frequency words, some of which do not match GPCs taught so far. If you have pupils in your class who are still struggling with the spelling of any of these words, it's worth looking back to your school's chosen SSP scheme and noting the order of teaching for these words. Prioritise pupils' learning of these words in that same order, as this is likely to be the vocabulary they will need most in their writing.

As pupils are taught the less common spelling alternatives to phonemes, many of the 'tricky' words become logical. The spellings of *love, eight* and *Christmas* are all unpicked alongside *month, weigh* and *chorus* in Year 3/4 spelling objectives, for example.

Within that list of common exception words, there remain many high-frequency words whose encryption seems to fly in the face of any spelling rule or convention. Because of their anomalies, these words will present difficulties to children throughout their time in primary education.

The word *yacht* is an interesting addition to the statutory list. In KS2 there is a list of 200 statutory words that the national curriculum believes pupils might frequently need but often misspell. I doubt the average primary pupil will require the word *yacht* every day, but it does exemplify the quirks of English spelling.

YACHT

I like to think of it as a barometer word – if children can spell *yacht*, they are probably feeling confident about spelling in general.

Why is it important to support learners to master these seemingly unconquerable words? Part of the answer lies in building pupils' overall accuracy and self-esteem. As these words represent a high proportion of common-use words, a pupil's writing will appear littered with mistakes if they haven't learned enough of them. Children are generally perceptive of their own strengths and weaknesses, and a pupil who makes errors in high-frequency words will often take a disproportionately dim view of their own capabilities. If pupils have not mastered these often-used words, cognitive load is taken up with encoding and this interrupts other transcriptional and compositional skills, making writing harder for the child.

Here are some practical ways that you can support pupils to internalise common exception words.

Isolate the 'tricky' part

Even the most exceptional spellings have some GPCs[4] that are predictable. Begin by asking the pupil to identify the parts of the word that are predictable: the 's' and 'd' in the word *said*, for instance. Map these onto a phoneme frame and add in the tricky part, perhaps in an alternative colour:

| s | ai | d |

Now support the pupil to focus on remembering the irregular part, perhaps using some of the following strategies:

Find analogies

Try to group words that share the target grapheme, such as:

he, me, she, we

could, should, would

wild, mild, child and *kind, find, mind*

---

4 grapheme- phoneme correspondence i.e. the relationship between the sound (phoneme) and the letter that represents it (grapheme)

This enables pupils to spot patterns in words and secure several words at once. Help the pupils to explore connections in meaning too, especially when there are distracting homophones in the mix: *here*, *there* and *where* all have a link to position, which might help pupils trying to select the correct spelling option; and the words *the*, *them* and *they* might support the spelling of the latter miscreant.

Explore mnemonics

The key to word mnemonics is to keep them simple and useful. Pupils may remember that 'big elephants can't always use small exits', but what if their spelling of *use* begins with the letter 'y' or the word *always* is also tricky for them? And pupils may find it hard to hold on to all seven words in that mnemonic while they construct the target word. Instead, focus the mnemonic on the tricky part of the word. Try to include the target word in the mnemonic to lessen cognitive load. For example, a memory trigger for the word *people* could be: **p**eople **e**at **o**melettes, **p**eople **l**ike **e**ggs. Sometimes a rhyme can help, such as 'there is no "a" in *they*'.

Self-regulation

Pupils need to take responsibility to 'seek and destroy' any words they should now spell correctly. Have a list of words for each year group, mistakes from which are 'past their sell-by date'. Words on this list become 'non-negotiable' and should be monitored by the pupil and self-corrected. Children can make a little bookmark for their writing books with a list of up to six words that they need to check. Once they have mastered a word, they can remove it from the bookmark and add another challenging word.

BUILD LIFE-LONG INDEPENDENCE

There is an adage that if you give someone a fish, you feed them for a day but teach them to fish and you feed them for life. Spelling teaching should be teaching children to spell for life, rather than giving them a list of spellings that they may retain for the short term and forget just as quickly. While pupils might struggle to remember hundreds of individual words, the more spelling strategies and conventions they know, the better they can self-serve and approach spelling with confidence and greater accuracy.

This knowledge is built through a robust teaching sequence where children are supported to review and connect prior knowledge to new spelling patterns. The emphasis needs to lie in teaching; practising should not dominate the lesson. Application is also key- children need to be encouraged to use what they have learned, to embed accurate spelling into their independent writing. And as with all skills, teachers need to model what that looks like.

> **ASIDE**
>
> Apart from the KS2 statutory lists, there is no direct prescription of word lists for pupils to be taught. Choose words within each spelling objective that match pupils' needs, interests and attainment.
>
> It's worth noting that the exact contents of the Year 1 and Year 2 lists are not statutory, and the national curriculum notes mention that other words could be included depending on the phonics and spelling programmes you use.
>
> Personally, I would add the word *does* and the numbers *one, two, four* and *eight*, as well as *Monday* and *Wednesday*.
>
> One of the reasons this is not a statutory list is that some of these words are perfectly regular in certain regional accents whereas their pronunciation in others renders them difficult to encode. For example, *past, last, fast, path* and *bath* are not exceptions in accents where the 'a' in these words is pronounced /æ/ as in *cat*.

ZEAL

Teachers who love teaching, teach children to love learning.

Unknown

You could liken the role of a teacher to that of an actor. From the minute you arrive in the building, you are warming up for your arrival on the stage that is the classroom. From that point, you stay in role for a marathon day-long show, after which there may be many fans or critics waiting at the stage door for a "quiet word".

Back at home, you rehearse your lines and prep for the next day's show. While you perform, you must not break role to give the audience a glimpse of your real opinion of fractions or statutory tests. Nor must you 'corpse' when a pupil does something that you internally chuckle about. The trademark of a good teacher is surely stage presence, including assembly voice, mock horror, feigned anger and unwavering zeal.

That zeal is key, even if you need to fake it at times. The show must go on day after day and year after year, whatever the political turmoil outside or personal heartache inside. As Albert Einstein once said, 'It is the supreme art of the teacher to awaken joy in creative expression and knowledge.'

For me, seeing children discover their own zest for learning is what re-inspires mine. Throughout this book I have detailed the complexities of the primary English curriculum. I've described the difficulties pupils – and teachers – might encounter as they build skills in language and literature. And I have shared the joy that is to be found in this area of our education.

What a privilege it is to teach English every day; to give children the keys to the castle of learning. Once they have mastered spoken language, reading and writing in English, children can unlock the door to any other area of the curriculum. Those doors open up into a world of amazing learning experiences that seek to inspire a life-long knowledge journey. On that journey, what gems are to be found in the glorious stories and poems written for young children! What excitement in taking part in increasingly sophisticated discussions as young minds formulate opinions and articulate them! And what pride is shared by pupils as they transcribe those thoughts using their burgeoning skills!

Not all of us arrive into the profession with a love of English studies. You might be a geography expert or lead maths. Your preference might not lie in reading poetry and you might not feel confident about teaching grammar. True, we all bring different strengths and expertise to the role. Pupils tend to know each teacher's passion: who will succumb if they beg for one more story versus who can be persuaded to stay outside for just one more game. However, for every one of us who has to plaster on a smile for football in the cold, there's another who must fake a love of reading aloud.

The 'fake it until you make it' approach is essential for English. Unarguably, English studies are the backbone of primary education. The skills acquired in the formative years will carry pupils through their entire education career, and by the time they leave primary, their attainment in reading and writing above all else will likely determine their future academic success. So we owe it to pupils to build confidence and develop enthusiasm for this aspect of the curriculum.

Practise reading that poem aloud until you have all the expression and passion of American poet Amanda Gorman. Summon that inner actor as you jump about demonstrating the difference an adverbial phrase can have on a sentence. Ooh and aah over the pupils' efforts to write a spine-chilling mystery. And make them believe that they can have the power to be great at English. The more you throw yourself into that mindset, the more your confidence will grow, until one day even the most determined hater of children's literature is recommending an amazing book they read over half term.

This book began with agency, and focused on the importance of creating a curriculum where children have a choice and a voice. Being able to have an aspect of control over their learning motivates pupils and engages them.

If pupils enjoy what they are reading, they carry on; if the book disappoints, they can swap it. This element of agency is also crucial for teachers. It may be trickier for our secondary colleagues: imagine having to teach *Romeo and Juliet* for 20 years. While the primary curriculum is detailed and prescriptive, and you may well have a long-term scheme or whole-school plan in place for English, there is room for autonomy and an element of choice.

If you don't especially love the book that is on the year group plan, within reason, see if you can swap it out. The key is a like-for-like swap: if the book has been chosen because it represents classic literature from our heritage, find another that fits the bill. If the selection has been made to introduce a particular theme or broaden the diversity of authors, don't choose something that undoes that roadmap. But literature is fast changing and there are so many fantastic books and authors emerging for our pupils to meet.

If we studied the same books year on year and didn't reflect on change, we'd all still only be teaching *Swallows and Amazons*, *The Secret Garden* or *The Tiger Who Came to Tea*.

What would *you* like to read to pupils and with pupils? And, importantly, what do you think they would enjoy reading or hearing? If pupils can hear your passion as you read, can hear your excitement as you discuss and feel the sadness when it comes to an end, you've succeeded. Our joy becomes their joy.

MOTIVATION

The reading-for-pleasure agenda is familiar and most schools aim to inspire a generation of volitional readers; life-long lovers of reading. Despite this, it seems that reading is less popular than ever before with children. In 2024, the National Literacy Trust (2024a) reported that only 34.6% of children and young people aged between 8 and 18 said they enjoyed reading in their spare time. This was the lowest figure recorded since their research began in 2005.

But what of writing for pleasure? Just as with reading, skills for writing need to be taught while nurturing the will. Without an interest or the enthusiasm to put pen to paper, how far can we expect quality – or even quantity – of outcomes? This policy seems less developed. Perhaps it feels harder, less natural. After all, how many adults would be able to cite the last time they wrote for pleasure? A comparative report by the National Literacy Trust (2024b) found that only 28.7% of children and young people surveyed enjoyed writing in their free time.

Despite the admirable championing being done by advocates such as the Open University, through their Reading for Pleasure initiative, the Writing for Pleasure Centre and teachers themselves, we all have our work cut out to inject zeal into the writing curriculum.

As mentioned in an earlier chapter, it may be that the term 'work' is the problem here. Pupils are forever trying to get on with their *work*, finish their *work* and they may often struggle with their *work*. Sometimes they confess that they are not enjoying their *work*. If we add 'lack of interest in the writing matter' or 'equating it to a chore' to any angst a pupil has around their ability to write, we have created a potentially fatal formula. So, what can be done to increase motivation and engagement in writing? A few quick suggestions are given here:

- Choose quality literature and film clips to ignite writing sequences. Create events and immersive moments that inspire pupils to respond in writing.
- Allow pupils to write about their lived experiences and interests and support them to know that their voice is valid and valued.
- Weave in an element of choice to writing units: yes, you want a persuasive argument as an outcome, but can the pupil choose the topic?
- Provide purposeful, pleasurable writing opportunities beyond tasks for 'units of work' (e.g. creating decorated labels for a display or writing a thank-you letter to the author of a book they enjoyed).

- Create a positive space for writing, where pupils receive plenty of encouragement and acknowledgement.
- Model the writing process and write frequently alongside pupils. Be the writer-teacher as well as the reader-teacher.
- Respond first and foremost to pupils' writing as an emotional reader. 'Wow, I could really picture the scene you described there!' or 'Gosh, that bit when the dragon entered gave me goosebumps!' rather than 'Don't forget to use full stops.'
- Publish the writing. Ensure pupils get to share the end result with their intended reader: a letter in the post, a class book, a performance.

However, the truth is that writing for pleasure, like its cousin reading for pleasure, will only come about if there is an appropriate culture within the school. Look for ways to make children the architects of literacy in their immediate and extended community. Writing the dinner menus, interviewing for a school newspaper, producing the script for the class assembly, contributing to book displays in the local library: these sorts of activities show them that reading and writing have a genuine purpose and audience beyond their teacher or their class peers.

CREATIVE EXPRESSION

Help pupils to see that learning to read and write is only part of a process, not an end point, by ensuring literacy lessons include drama, performance, debate, visual arts. These areas should not be bolted on or only squeezed in if time allows. Each provides an outlet for artistic expression while simultaneously building creative skills.

Drama is vital for fostering creativity, communication and collaboration. It helps pupils develop confidence as they explore learning through role play and performance. It also enhances emotional intelligence by encouraging empathy and understanding of diverse perspectives. But beyond personal growth, drama enriches language development and supports literacy through vocabulary expansion and storytelling techniques.

Providing pupils with opportunities to represent their ideas through or alongside artwork is similarly motivating. Children who might lack the confidence to communicate through writing can often feel inspired when encouraged to illustrate their writing or use a medium such as the graphic novel to convey their ideas.

Knowing they are aiming for a polished, published version of their writing, designed to engage a genuine audience, can be the spark that fires pupils to give their very best. The positive reception of their efforts is its own reward and will generally further inspire. If pupils find it difficult to create their own artwork, the internet can certainly supply or generate what they need.

EMBRACE THE FUTURE

Technology progresses at a rapid pace, but it's an integral part of children's lives now. According to the British Council (n.d.), the UK's gaming industry is the sixth largest in the world with around 32 million people playing games and, at the point of writing, over 200 related courses are now available to undergraduates.

Rather than try to compete for children's attention, harness their enthusiasm in this area. The modern literacy curriculum needs to appear relevant and build skills in readiness for pupils' future employment. Technology is with us and ready for the taking: spelling apps on tablets, electronic versions of books, software for publishing writing, performing against a green screen, speech-to-text recognition to aid composition, AI-generated images to create tailored illustrations. Embrace the future and incorporate it into English teaching.

> ## ASIDE
> ### LIFE-LONG ZEAL
> Even when you love English as a curriculum subject and welcome all the creativity it affords, you can sometimes feel that zeal being crushed by the weight of expectations. Primary teaching is as relentless as it is rewarding. But teachers are generally selfless and you don't need to look far to discover someone injecting a new idea into English teaching, sharing a stunning display or recommending a great new book.
>
> There are many friendly groups on social media offering everything from subject-leader support to book groups. If you prefer to stay away from online sites, ask around to see if there is a group that meets in person to support and inspire. Trusts often have their own network of English leads, as do some geographical areas, but if you can't find one, set something up!
>
> English is the bedrock of primary education, equipping pupils with skills and inspiration that extend far beyond the classroom. Keeping that zeal alive in yourself is key to pupils' success in the subject. Passionate teaching transforms English from a subject to an experience, where students discover the joy of words, the power of storytelling and the beauty of expression. And children who love learning inspire teachers.

SECTION TWO

BIBLIOPHAGE

BOOK RECOMMENDATIONS: IDEAS TO TRY IN CLASS

1. Teacher-to-pupil personal suggestions work well. The biggest privilege of all might be to be lent a personal copy of a book by the class teacher or the headteacher. I used to love reading the opening to a book and stopping at a cliffhanger or just as events are about to take off. Then I would pop it to one side and provide a sign-up sheet for whomever wanted to take it home next. This should grow to work both ways; it's a very special thing when a pupil (especially if they have been a reluctant reader in the past) recommends a book that they think *you* would like. It is so important to follow through and make time to discuss what you thought of it.

2. Peer-to-peer recommendations are powerful too: who better to know what you might like than a friend?

   - Provide opportunities for pupils to talk informally to classmates about a book they are enjoying and read a little of it to an individual or group. Everyone loves a personal recommendation.
   - Pupils could wrap books and add a label with another child's name on it saying, 'Lucca, I enjoyed this and thought that you might want to read it next, because the main character reminds me of you. From Max.'
   - Take a picture of each pupil holding their favourite book and attach a short summary by the pupil explaining why this book is so special.

3. Purchase duplicate copies of some books so that pupils can pair read and discuss a book with a friend. You don't even need to devote large chunks of time to this if you build a book buzz whereby children can respond when you say, 'As you come and sit on the carpet, tell your talk partner the name of the book you have enjoyed most this month' or 'As you go out to play, tag someone with a book recommendation.' Pupils should also be able to suggest recommendations for the class library, so why not produce a wish list that they can add to?

4. This activity works a bit like 'speed dating': half the class sit arranged in an inner circle with the rest of the class sat facing them in an outer circle. The pairs have two minutes to present each other with details of a book they have recently enjoyed. If there is time, they can read a little section. At the end of the two minutes, the pupils in the outer circle get up and move around one place. When the children are back to their original places, each pupil can select the book(s) they would most like to read next.

EDITING

MODELLING EDITING WITH COMMENTARY

Additions: adding words, sentences or even sections to improve detail and enhance the reader's understanding.		
Draft	**Edit**	**Commentary**
Mia had a ball. >	Mia had a red ball.	'If I tell the reader the colour of the ball, they can picture it in their minds. I could also tell them it's a giant red ball. Can you imagine it now?'
The wolf was arrested. >	The wolf was arrested for impersonating an old lady.	'My reader needs to know why the wolf was arrested, so I'll add that information to the end of my sentence.'

Removals: removing words, phrases and even whole sections that repeat information, express something in an overly wordy way or add unnecessary detail that slows the pace for the reader and might cause them to lack interest.		
Draft	**Edit**	**Commentary**
The big, grey, lonely elephant lived in the jungle. >	The lonely elephant lived in the jungle.	'I think my reader will know that the elephant is big and grey because all elephants are big and grey. I'll take that out and leave *lonely* because that is the important thing about the elephant in my story.'

THE A–Z OF PRIMARY ENGLISH

Draft	Edit	Commentary
Little Red Riding Hood, who was 11 years old at the time of the incident, was terrified by the awful ordeal. >	Little Red Riding Hood, who was 11, was terrified by the ordeal.	'This relative clause "who was 11 years old at the time of the incident" adds helpful extra information, but I can say it more concisely > "who was 11" says the same thing. I don't need the phrase "at the time of the incident"; that is implied. Is there another word I can remove? *Awful*. *Ordeal* means an awful experience. I think this sentence flows better now; it doesn't slow down the story.'

Moves: swapping the order of information or moving sections that more logically sit somewhere else. This might make the writing flow better and enhance the reader's enjoyment. Individual words might have more impact if moved elsewhere in the sentence.

Draft	Edit	Commentary
Zak had a bad dream and he was asleep. >	Zak was asleep and he had a bad dream.	'I think I need to change the order in which I give the reader my information: "and he was asleep" doesn't sound quite right. Zak went to sleep and then he had a bad dream while he was asleep.'
Valentina Tereshkova flew a solo mission into space in 1963 and orbited the Earth 48 times. She was the first woman in space. >	Valentina Tereshkova was the first woman in space. She flew a solo mission into space in 1963 and orbited the Earth 48 times.	'I need to start with the most significant piece of information first: what is Valentina famed for? Then I can add the details after that. Read the second sentence. Is there any other piece of information that might benefit from moving? Yes, we can move the date to the beginning of the sentence to link it to the preceding fact. (And we can lose the repetition of "in space" to make the information more succinct for the reader.)'

Substitutions: would another word sound better here or add precision to the information?		
Draft	**Edit**	**Commentary**
Goldilocks lived in a house. >	Goldilocks lived in a cottage.	'A cottage is a pretty little house, often found in the countryside.'
The field was covered in tiny, white flowers. >	The meadow was littered with daisies.	'A meadow is a grassy area. I have used the word *field* elsewhere, so I'll say *meadow* this time. A daisy is a little, white flower that often grows in grass. I can use a specific noun to help my reader picture the flower.'

EDITING STRATEGIES

Try these specific strategies for helping pupils to edit effectively and independently:

Editing flaps

Break the editing process up for pupils by asking them to pick one paragraph to edit. Pupils can then take a separate strip of lined paper and re-draft and improve this one paragraph to make it stand out as an example. Once they have finished re-drafting the paragraph, the paper can be cut out and glued – only at the margin – into their book so that it forms a flap over the original paragraph.

Why this works:

- It can be a daunting task to edit a whole text, so this breaks it down for pupils by getting them to pick one paragraph at a time to edit.
- Having the new strip of paper gives them space to fully re-draft the content and the syntax of their work rather than making minuscule, illegible corrections above their writing or in the margin.

Wiggly line spellings

As pupils are writing their first draft, ask them to draw a thin, wiggly line underneath any spellings that they are unsure about. They can later locate words they wish to check in a dictionary during the proofreading process.

Why this works:

- It allows pupils to write without losing their train of thought.
- Pupils are more likely to be ambitious with their word choices if they know they can return to the word later to check its spelling (and meaning) without stopping mid-sentence to do so.

Editing stations

Different tables can be set up for different purposes – perhaps using the 'cups' model; each table or station will focus on one aspect of the success criteria. Pupils visit a table at a time and follow the instructions at the table.

Why this works:

- Simply giving pupils the chance to stretch their legs when moving between tables and discuss their writing with multiple peers can help them to see their writing afresh.
- Pupils are given time to focus on each part of the success criteria individually rather than feeling overwhelmed by an intimidating list of features they need to check in their writing.

Signposting

Instead of underlining/highlighting an error made by the pupil, place an asterisk in the margin; use one asterisk for every error they have made on that line.

Why this works:

- Pupils become more active editors. By searching for their own errors, they become less reliant on you as their teacher to pick up on every mistake they make. As a result, they become well practised in reviewing their own work.
- It is a good way of gradually removing direct support from pupils who are used to an adult directing their editing and proofreading.

Seek and destroy

At the end of a lesson, play a motivational piece of music for two minutes. During this time, the pupils need to read through their writing and seek out as many spelling or punctuation errors as possible.

Why this works:

- Pupils become active proofreaders – the onus is on them to spot mistakes in the first instance rather than relying on an adult to provide 'corrections'.
- Pupils focus their attention for a set period and look out for the errors that they could have self-corrected. That means your feedback can concentrate on misconceptions.

PROOFREADING ACTIVITY

Present the pupils with a piece of text that is littered with punctuation and spelling errors. Ask them to find the mistakes and correct them. They find it easier to do this on something they haven't written.

Alternatively, turn it into a game and pit yourself against the class. The pupils must find as many mistakes as they can. As they spot a mistake, draw in a body part for a snowman, such as the one below. Initially, they will find a few low-hanging fruit, but, as the mistakes get harder to spot, remove parts of the snowman from the board if they make an incorrect suggestion or if a minute passes without a suggested correction. Can they save the snowman from disappearing by identifying all the mistakes?

Snowman

can we go to the them park asked gemma no its to expnsive said mum. Then mum looks in her perse and smiles i tell you what she announcd exitedly. we can visit the local zoo i have to vouchers hear and they say were aloud to go in for harf price on wenesday luckily it was Wenesday so that was a usefull find Gemma and her mum packd a lunch and hurryed of to get the next bus. Unforchunately it was late so they dident get to the zoo untill ¼ parst 2 Despite that she hasn't got the theme park Gemma had a amazing time

FLUENCY PROMPTS

During reading practice, offer clear, specific feedback designed to praise progress and provide constructive prompts:

- 'Some good expression there; you read this part like this. How would you show me with your voice which words are important here?'
- 'You sounded good to listen to there. Shall we go back to the beginning of this page and read the whole section like that?'
- 'You blended each of those words well. Now let's scoop up those three words because they make a sentence as a group.'
- 'Well done – you read each word accurately. Now go back to the beginning of the sentence and put all the words together.'
- 'That's definitely sounding smoother. Go back to the start of the sentence and read it a little faster – at talking speed.'
- 'Wow! You read that sentence with no mistakes. Try reading it again but slow down a little.'
- 'I like how you got louder when it said, "Jack shouted". How would you read this part where they are whispering?'

HANDWRITING

BUILDING BETTER HANDWRITING

A number of factors can take their toll on a young writer: poor positioning of the pupil or paper, poor pen grip and incorrect letter formation leading to inefficiencies of script. The actual letter formation can be hardest to address. Try these strategies:

Small steps

Support the pupil to improve letter by letter. It may feel as if this would take 26 weeks, but it really does have a snowball effect. Identify one or two letters that the pupil is consistently writing incorrectly, either in terms of form, sizing or placement on the line. Model the letter formation, explaining what you are looking out for, for example, 'The ascender for the "h" needs to be nice and tall rather than the same size as the ascender for the "n", so that we can tell the difference.' Then, the child practises with the teacher and is given feedback.

Challenge the pupil to start each piece of work with a row of these letters. Which ones are they proud of? Underline or circle them and then complete writing tasks with special attention paid to the letters practised. In this example, the teacher places a few examples in the Year 1 pupil's book for them to practise before they begin the rest of their writing task.

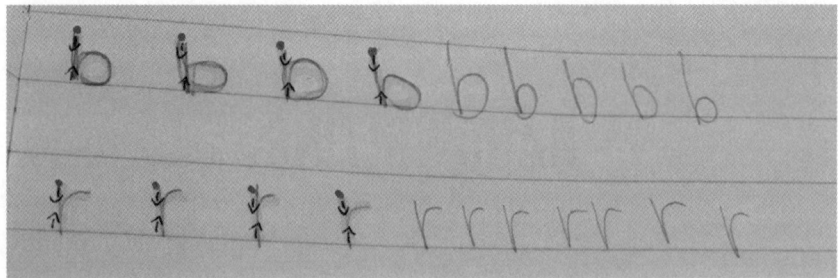

Review writing and check letter formation of target letters: which need fixing, and which ones match the expectation? Continue each week with a new letter, recording the previously addressed letters on a bookmark as a reminder for the pupil. The following week, the pupil and teacher select another letter formation to work on; again, this will be self-monitored by the pupil. Hopefully the previous week's letter is embedded, but this can be checked from time to time to ensure old habits are not revisited.

The pupil's bookmark could reference letters to check so far and help pupils understand what to look out for: do tall letters all have clear ascenders; does the lower-case 'p' sit with its body on the line and descender underneath; are the letters 'c' and 's' correctly sized depending on whether they are upper case or lower case, and so on? As the weeks go on, the worst letter formation will have been addressed and you may notice that the handwriting looks a lot better in general. Further individual attention on letters may not be needed at all, or could be addressed in groups, for example, 'Ensure descenders don't loop down into the letters on the line below.'

Look at the following example from a child in Year 2. Support correct formation of the letter 'k' here: it's a commonly used letter and perhaps the most malformed. Ensure it stands taller than the small letters without ascenders. Then in week two, look to address the height of a couple more letters with ascenders such as l and h. In the third week you might focus on raising the height of the remaining tall letters before turning attention to lower-case y and g. Lines would help here but the issues of size, positioning and formation tend to exist regardless. Nevertheless, by supporting the child with small, manageable changes, impact should be seen within three to four weeks.

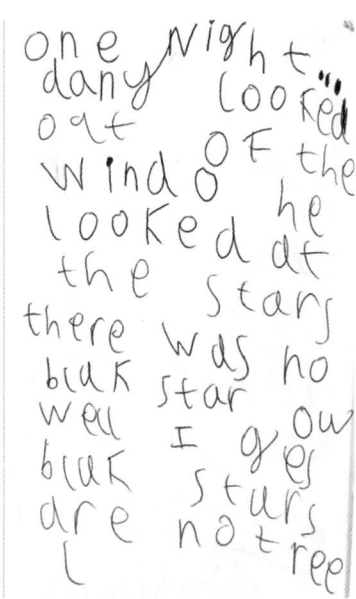

'The gold standard'

Work with a pupil to identify a piece of work they are proud of in terms of handwriting and presentation (not handwriting practice). Photocopy the piece of work and stick it into the cover of the pupil's book as a pull-out flap that they can open up whenever they start a new piece of work. This is their own 'gold standard' below which they would not wish to drop. When the pupil feels that they can consistently match or improve on this standard, they may choose a new gold standard to replace the original piece of writing and use the new piece as their personal benchmark.

This process is repeated through the year and avoids inconsistencies of presentation.

MODELS

CHANGING ONE VARIABLE

When producing sentence models for writing support, I often look to the techniques used in foreign language tuition. The 'change one variable' strategy, for example, is particularly useful for younger pupils or those new to English where a formulaic approach to initial sentence building develops confidence and fluency.

I can vividly remember a French lesson where we learned to list the items in our pencil case. We were all able to create multiple accurate sentences having pre-learned the names of the various bits of classroom stationery. The set phrase *'Dans ma trousse il y a …'* could be followed by naming one of the objects. In each case, the variable was the item of stationery and the sentence stem remained constant. Try this with sentence openers such as:

My teddy bear has …

I like pizza and …

then

I like rice but not …

Or change two variables:

_____ *are made of* _____.

On _____ *the hungry caterpillar ate a* _____ . (In the style of Eric Carle's *The Very Hungry Caterpillar.*)

THE FADED SCAFFOLD PRINCIPLE

The principle of a faded scaffold is perfect for building stamina and confidence in the early stages of independent writing. Like the 'change one variable' approach, security is provided by familiarity and repetition. Composition and creativity are minimal; the emphasis is on fluency and internalising the grammatical structure.

A pupil is given a fully worked model of a sentence and several more underneath that remove a word at a time until the pupil is writing the complete sentence themselves.

For example:

At playtime

I like to skip.

I like to_____

I like _____

I _____

_____

By the end of the session, the pupil has written four sentences and each one takes them on a journey to independence.

Modelling Spelling

Support children's application of spelling by incorporating spelling patterns that you have taught into your writing models. Here is an example using the Y5/6 objective 'words ending with -tious or -cious':

Jamie was an <u>ambitious</u> teenager. Nowadays everyone loves his <u>delicious</u> recipes, which are always designed to be <u>nutritious</u>.

ORACY

Try these activities:

ENCOURAGING INVOLVEMENT

While it's vital to get every pupil joining in, certain activities – like 'lollipop stick pickers' – can create anxiety if not well integrated. Here are effective alternatives to ensure all pupils are busy thinking and building confidence to join in:

- **Thinking time**: Allow time to think, plan and write before sharing with a partner or group. This is also an ideal moment for adult support.
- **'Show me, don't tell me'**: Use mini-whiteboards, response cards, hand gestures or classroom polls to encourage non-verbal responses.
- **Talk tokens or talk towers**: Each pupil has tokens to submit or bricks to stack when speaking. This encourages quieter students to participate and active talkers to share thoughtfully.
- **Talk detectives**: Assign quieter students a role to observe and monitor group discussions, helping them engage without pressure to speak.
- **Four corners**: Pose a question with multiple-choice answers, assigning each option a corner of the room. Students move to their answer's corner, encouraging movement and discussion.
- **ABC**: Encourage listening and effective response using ABC. All responses must Add to, Build upon or Challenge the other speaker. This is useful for reflecting on responses.

CIRCLE TIME

The 'circle time' approach, developed by Jenny Mosley, works with all age groups and builds social skills as well as spoken language skills. It is a very controlled, structured way into group participation, building pupils' self-esteem and fostering mutual respect. Pupils sit in a circle (start with groups, build to whole class) so that they can see and hear everyone in the group.

A task is set, ranging from a simple question such as 'What is your favourite colour?' to 'Tell me about a time when someone was kind to you this week' or even 'Give one reason for or against school uniform.' Pupils take it in turns to respond briefly until everyone in the group has had the opportunity to give an answer. Teachers can model an example of a response using a complete sentence.

There are few rules, but they are consistently applied to each session. An item symbolising a conch shell (such as a bean bag or class mascot) is passed around and the only person allowed to speak is the one holding the item. Pupils pass the 'conch' to the child sitting next to them, who may choose to pass if they do not feel they can give an answer. At the end of the round, any pupils who passed have a second chance to respond if they wish.

SPELLING: ACCURACY WITH COMMON EXCEPTION WORDS

Here are some practical ways that you can support pupils to internalise common exception words.

TEACH OFTEN

Frequent usage should suggest frequent teaching and yet these words are perhaps not revisited enough in lessons. KS2 pupils still need to be taught strategies to support them to learn and remember these words. Gaps in KS1 spelling knowledge are a blocker to meeting the expectations for writing at the end of Year 6. Testing alone will not help, but spaced recall is important. Include these words on a regular basis so that they move from the short-term memory to the long-term memory.

GROW AUTOMATICITY

'Sight' learning is not a helpful strategy. Because there are so many words, often similar in appearance, most pupils won't be able to memorise many spellings in this way. However, overlearning, with a view to automaticity, is the key. Constant revisiting and writing of these words will cement the spelling, creating an unconscious habit that is the result of visual familiarity and muscle memory. So, set the pupils challenges such as 'How many times can you write the word in joined handwriting in one minute?' or 'Can you spell this word with your eyes closed?' It can be fun to set passwords on IT equipment as commonly misspelled words to encourage accuracy!

MONITOR CONSTANTLY

If a word is used frequently and misspelled from the outset, it won't be long before a mistake turns into a habit. Ensure errors in high-frequency words are addressed promptly. If a Year 1 pupil spells the word *they* with an 'a' five times in one week – or even in one piece of writing – and it isn't picked up immediately, the chances are you'll still be battling to undo that muscle memory in Year 5! Point out these inaccuracies from the outset and then have high expectations as a school for the correct spelling of this word moving forward.

VERSE

Try these ideas:

- List poems can be as simple as:

My dog can
Bark
Jump
Sniff
Run ...

Green is
The grass
A pea
A bush
My book

- Repetition poems – such as Julia Donaldson's *The Food Train* – can provide an easily replicable structure for young children. Even simple sentences can be transformed into poetry:

I can jump
Jump jump jump
I can hop
Hop hop hop
I can clap
Clap clap clap ...

- Soundscapes for onomatopoeia such as 'The garden at night' or 'Out on my street'.
- Structural poems such as cinquains (poems with five lines) that focus on counting syllables rather than rhyming.
- Kennings, which have a simple, tight, replicable structure. Kate Wakeling's *Stick Insect* is a great example.
- Use the layout of other forms of writing to create a framework with a play on words. Procedural writing works well: 'A recipe for friendship' or 'Instructions for laughter'.
- Use the format of existing poems as a scaffold to adapt, swapping out some of the poet's words for the children's own. Examples that work well are Kit Wright's *The Magic Box* or Roger McGough's *The Sound Collector*.
- Use the concept of existing poems to inspire a similarly structured poem. For example, instead of *The Sea Is a Hungry Dog*, pupils could create an extended metaphor for 'The Sun is an angry lion' or 'The Moon is a snow-white owl'.
- Create group performance poems where each pupil contributes a line, such as phrases heard on the playground ('Playground rap') or lines of alliteration based on different animals ('Amazing alliterative animals').

VOCABULARY AND MORPHOLOGY

Try these investigations with pupils to build their vocabulary as well as their spelling prowess:

1. Use your knowledge of affixes to create pairs or opposite words such as *social/antisocial* or *possible/impossible*. Explain the meaning of each word. Can you invent any new pairs based on your spelling and vocabulary knowledge, e.g. *submarine/supermarine*?
2. Create chains of similar words and give the meanings of each word. Challenge: identify the root word and find out its original meaning. For example, here the word *point* means 'the sense, the matter' as in 'what's the point?' How does that link the words?

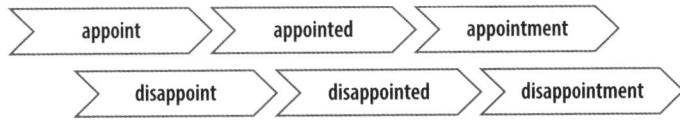

3. Choose a root word (base morpheme) and a few words that use that morpheme plus one other. Challenge the pupils to a) find a word that shares the other morpheme and b) write the meaning of each word built from the central root. For example, the first one here could be *telephone* meaning 'sound over a distance' and *television* meaning 'sight over a distance'.

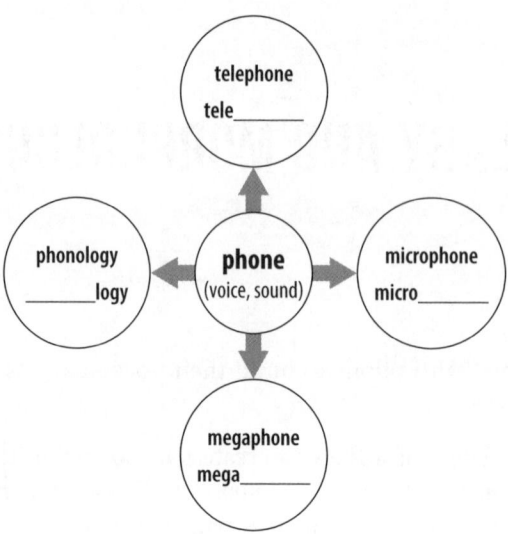

4. If you know x, what else do you know? Set a challenge for pupils to find as many words derived from one root as possible (in a mixed-attainment table group/for a homework investigation). For example, the Latin verb *vertere* means 'to turn' and in English we see a form of the verb in words ending -verse or -vert, such as *advert* or *converse*. If you know this, how many words can you think of that contain this root word? What do they mean? Challenge: use your knowledge of affixes to derive the literal meaning of each word. For example, *ad* means 'to', so an advert is where you turn someone to you (or your ideas). Why might the word *universe* have been given its name?

REFERENCES

Bandura, A.J. (1977). *Social Learning Theory*. Englewood Cliffs, NJ: Prentice Hall.

Barnes, D., Britton, J. & Rosen, H. (1971). *Language, the Learner and the School*. London: Penguin Books.

Beck, I.L., McKeown, M.G. & Kucan, L. (2013). *Bringing Words to Life: Robust Vocabulary Instruction*. New York: Guilford Press.

Book Trust. (2022). 'Life-changing libraries: report 2022'. Available at: www.booktrust.org.uk/globalassets/resources/life-changing-libraries/life-changing-libraries-report---final.pdf

British Council. (n.d.). 'Study gaming in the UK'. Available at: https://study-uk.britishcouncil.org/plan-studies/choosing-course/subjects/gaming

Britton, J. (1983). 'Writing and the story of the world'. In B.M. Kroll & C.G. Wells (Eds), *Explorations in the Development of Writing: Theory, Research, and Practice* (pp. 3–30). New York, NY: Wiley.

Centre for Literacy in Primary Education (CLPE) & Macmillan Children's Books. (2023). 'Poetry in primary schools 2023'. Available at: https://clpe.org.uk/system/files/2023-03/CLPE%20Poetry%20Survey%202023.pdf

Centre for Literacy in Primary Education (CLPE). (2024). 'Reflecting realities: Survey of ethnic representation within UK children's literature'. Available at: https://clpe.org.uk/research/clpe-reflecting-realities-survey-ethnic-representation-within-uk-childrens-literature-2

Chambers, A. (1996). *Tell Me (Children, Reading and Talk) with the Reading Environment*. London: Routledge.

Cremin, T. (2019). 'Reading communities: why, what and how?'. *Primary Matters,* published by the National Association for the Teaching of English (NATE), Summer 2019. Available at: www.nate.org.uk/wp-content/uploads/2020/03/4-Reading-Communities-Teresa-Cremin.pdf

Crystal, D. (2013). *Spell It Out: The Curious, Enthralling and Extraordinary Story of English Spelling*. New York: St Martin's Press.

Csikszentmihalyi, M. (2008). *Flow: The Psychology of Optimal Experience*. New York: Harper Perennial.

Department for Education. (2013a). 'English programmes of study: Key stages 1 and 2 (National curriculum in England)'. Available at: https://assets.publishing.service.gov.uk/media/5a7de93840f0b62305b7f8ee/PRIMARY_national_curriculum_-_English_220714.pdf

Department for Education. (2013b). 'The national curriculum in England: Key stages 1 and 2 framework document'. Available at: https://assets.publishing.service.gov.uk/media/5a81a9abe5274a2e8ab55319/PRIMARY_national_curriculum.pdf

Department for Education. (2019). 'School inspection update: Special edition, January 2019'. Available at: https://assets.publishing.service.gov.uk/media/5c41e555ed915d38a6a87aeb/School_inspection_update_-_January_2019_Special_Edition_180119.pdf

Department for Education. (2023a). 'The reading framework'. Available at: https://assets.publishing.service.gov.uk/media/664f600c05e5fe28788fc437/The_reading_framework_.pdf

Department for Education. (2023b). 'Validation of systematic synthetic phonics programmes: supporting documentation'. Available at: www.gov.uk/government/publications/phonics-teaching-materials-core-criteria-and-self-assessment/validation-of-systematic-synthetic-phonics-programmes-supporting-documentation

Department for Education. (2024a). 'Key stage 2 attainment: National headlines'. Available at: https://explore-education-statistics.service.gov.uk/find-statistics/key-stage-2-attainment-national-headlines

Department for Education. (2024b). 'Special educational needs in England'. Available at: https://explore-education-statistics.service.gov.uk/find-statistics/special-educational-needs-in-england

Department for Education. (2024c). 'Early years foundation stage profile results'. Available at: https://explore-education-statistics.service.gov.uk/find-statistics/early-years-foundation-stage-profile-results

Department for Education and Department of Health. (2015). 'Special educational needs and disability code of practice: 0 to 25 years'. Available at: https://assets.publishing.service.gov.uk/media/5a7dcb85ed915d2ac884d995/SEND_Code_of_Practice_January_2015.pdf

Department for Statistics of England & Wales. (2022). '2021 Census'. Available at: www.ethnicity-facts-figures.service.gov.uk/uk-population-by-ethnicity/national-and-regional-populations/population-of-england-and-wales/latest/

Department for Work and Pensions. (2024). 'Households below average income: an analysis of the UK income distribution: FYE 1995 to FYE 2023'. Available at: www.gov.uk/government/statistics/households-below-average-income-for-financial-years-ending-1995-to-2023/households-below-average-income-an-analysis-of-the-uk-income-distribution-fye-1995-to-fye-2023

Education Endowment Foundation. (2021). 'Special educational needs in mainstream schools'. Available at: https://educationendowmentfoundation.org.uk/education-evidence/guidance-reports/send

Education Endowment Foundation. (2024). 'EEF blog: Five-a-day for pupils with SEND – a cluster of adaptive approaches'. Available at: https://educationendowmentfoundation.org.uk/news/eef-blog-five-a-day-for-pupils-with-send-a-cluster-of-adaptive-approaches

Fitts, P.M. & Posner, M.I. (1967). *Human Performance*. Belmont, CA: Brooks/Cole.

Gandhi, M.K. (1929). *Autobiography: The Story of My Experiments with Truth*. Ahmedabad, India: Navajivan Trust.

Goldberg, N. (2005). *Writing Down the Bones: Freeing the Writer Within*. Boulder: Shambhala Publications Inc.

Gough, P.B. & Tunmer, W.E. (1986). 'Decoding, reading, and reading disability'. *Remedial and Special Education*, 7(1), pp. 6–10. Available at: https://doi.org/10.1177/074193258600700104

Gov.UK. (2024). 'Early years foundation stage profile results: Academic year 2023/24'. Available at: https://explore-education-statistics.service.gov.uk/find-statistics/early-years-foundation-stage-profile-results

Hanna, P.R., Hodges, R.E., Hanna, J.S. & Rudorf, E.H. Jr. (1966). *Phoneme–Grapheme Correspondences as Cues to Spelling Improvement.* Washington, DC: US Department of Health, Education, and Welfare, Office of Education.

Hart, B. & Risley, T.R. (1995). *Meaningful Differences in the Everyday Experience of Young American Children.* Baltimore, MD: Brookes Publishing.

Hattie, J. & Yates, G.C.R. (2013). *Visible Learning and the Science of How We Learn.* London: Routledge.

House of Commons Library. (2024). 'UK disability statistics: Prevalence and life experiences'. Available at: https://commonslibrary.parliament.uk/research-briefings/cbp-9602

Hulme, P. (n.d.). 'Teaching fully cursive writing in Reception'. National Handwriting Association. Available at: https://nha-handwriting.org.uk/handwriting/articles/teaching-fully-cursive-writing-in-reception/

Levin, T. & Long, R. (1981). 'Effective instruction'. *Review of Educational Research,* 51(1), pp. 233–270.

Mercer, N. (n.d.). 'Why teach oracy?'. Available at: www.cam.ac.uk/research/discussion/why-teach-oracy?

Montessori, M. (1967). *The Absorbent Mind.* (C.A. Claremont, Trans.) New York, NY: Holt, Rinehart, and Winston.

Mosley, J. (1989). *All-Round Success.* Trowbridge: Wiltshire Local Education Authority. (Jenny Mosley Consultancies, available at: www.circle-time.co.uk/review-research-underpins-jenny-mosleys-quality-circle-time-circles-support-model/)

Myatt, M. (2022). 'Curriculum 101: Sequencing the curriculum'. (blog: 8 October 2022). Available at: https://marymyatt.substack.com/p/sequencing-the-curriculum

Myhill, D., Jones, S., Watson, A. & Lines, H. (2016). *Essential Primary Grammar.* Maidenhead: Open University Press.

National Literacy Trust. (2024a). 'Children and young people's reading in 2024'. Available at: https://literacytrust.org.uk/research-services/research-reports/children-and-young-peoples-reading-in-2024/

National Literacy Trust. (2024b). 'Children and young people's writing in 2024'. Available at: https://literacytrust.org.uk/research-services/research-reports/children-and-young-peoples-writing-in-2024/

National Literacy Trust. (2024c). 'Parents' support for young children's literacy at home in 2024'. Available at: https://nlt.cdn.ngo/media/documents/Parents_support_for_young_childrens_literacy_at_home_in_2024.pdf

National Literacy Trust. (2024d). 'Book ownership in 2024'. Available at: https://literacytrust.org.uk/research-services/research-reports/book-ownership-in-2024/

National Trust. (2013). 'Children's and young people's reading in 2012'. Available at: https://literacytrust.org.uk/research-services/research-reports/childrens-and-young-peoples-reading-2012/

Nicholls, D. (2022a). 'Closing the disadvantage gap: Curriculum as the lever'. (blog: 11 February 2022). Available at: https://dannicholls1.com/2022/02/11/disadvantage-gap-curriculum-as-the-lever/

Nicholls, D. (2022b). 'The world is getting darker: Bringing light to those who need it most'. (blog: 10 October 2022). Available at: https://dannicholls1.com/2022/10/10/the-world-is-getting-darker-bring-light/

Ofsted. (2019). 'School inspection update: Special edition, January 2019'. Available at: https://assets.publishing.service.gov.uk/media/5c41e555ed915d38a6a87aeb/School_inspection_update_-_January_2019_Special_Edition_180119.pdf

Ofsted. (2024). 'Telling the story: The English education subject report'. Available at: www.gov.uk/government/publications/subject-report-series-english/telling-the-story-the-english-education-subject-report

Oracy Education Commission. (2024). 'We need to talk: The report of the Commission on the Future of Oracy Education in England'. Available at: https://oracyeducationcommission.co.uk/wp-content/uploads/2024/10/We-need-to-talk-2024.pdf

Oxford University Press. (2023). 'Oxford language report 2023: Building children's vocabulary'. Available at: https://home.oxfordowl.co.uk/the-oxford-language-report-building-vocabulary/

Pennac, D. (2006). *The Rights of the Reader*. London: Walker Books Ltd.

Rasinski, T.V. (2012). 'Why reading fluency should be hot!'. *The Reading Teacher*, 65(8), pp. 516–522.

Rosenshine, B. (2012). 'Principles of instruction: Research-based strategies that all teachers should know'. *American Educator*, 36. Available at: www.aft.org/sites/default/files/Rosenshine.pdf

Samuels, S.J. (1979). 'The method of repeated readings'. *The Reading Teacher*, 32, pp. 403–408.

Scarborough, H.S., Fletcher-Campbell, F., Soler, J.M. & Reid, G. (2001). 'Connecting early language and literacy to later reading (dis)abilities: Evidence, theory, and practice'. In S.B. Neuman & D.K. Dickinson (Eds), *Handbook of Early Literacy Research* (pp. 97–110). New York: Guilford Press.

Sims Bishop, R. (1990). 'Mirrors, windows, and sliding glass doors'. Originally published in *Perspectives: Choosing and Using Books from the Classroom*, 6(3) (Summer 1990). Available at: https://scenicregional.org/wp-content/uploads/2017/08/Mirrors-Windows-and-Sliding-Glass-Doors.pdf

Smith, J. (2011). 'The rights of the writer'. Available at: https://thenationalwritingproject.weebly.com/uploads/5/7/5/2/57522719/poster_right_to_write2_1.pdf

Sobel, D. (2018). *Narrowing the Attainment Gap: A Handbook for Schools*. London: Bloomsbury Publishing.

Standards & Testing Agency. (2017). 'Non-statutory teacher assessment frameworks at the end of key stage 1: Guidance'. Gov.UK. Updated version available at: www.gov.uk/government/publications/teacher-assessment-frameworks-at-the-end-of-key-stage-1/non-statutory-teacher-assessment-frameworks-at-the-end-of-key-stage-1

Standards & Testing Agency. (2018). 'Teacher assessment frameworks at the end of key stage 2'. Gov.UK. Available at: https://assets.publishing.service.gov.uk/media/637ba0b0e90e072854bcab87/2018-19_teacher_assessment_frameworks_at_the_end_of_key_stage_2.pdf

Truss, L. (2009). *Eats, Shoots & Leaves*. London: Harper Collins.

Vygotsky, L.S. (1978). *Mind in Society: The Development of Higher Psychological Processes*. (M. Cole, V. John-Steiner, S. Scribner & E. Souberman, Eds). Cambridge, MA: Harvard University Press.

Wiliam, D. (2017). *Embedded Formative Assessment*. Bloomington, IN: Solution Tree Press.

Wilkinson, A., Davies, A. & Atkinson, D. (1965). *Spoken English*. Oxford: Oxford University Press.

Wolf, M. (2008). *Proust and the Squid: The Story and Science of the Reading Brain*. Cambridge: Icon Books Ltd.

The A–Z series focuses on the 'fun and fundamentals' of what's happening in primary, special and secondary schools today. Each title is written by a leading practitioner, adopting a series approach of reflection, advice and provocation.

As a group of authors with a strong belief in the power of education to shape and change young people's lives, we hope teachers and leaders in the UK and internationally enjoy what we have to say.

Roy Blatchford, series editor

The A–Z of Great Classrooms (2023)
The A–Z of Secondary Leadership (2023)
The A–Z of Primary Maths (2024)
The A–Z of School Improvement (2024)
The A–Z of Diversity and Inclusion (2024)
The A–Z of Trust Leadership (2024)
The A–Z of International School Leadership (2024)
The A–Z of Special Educational Needs (2024)
The A–Z of Early Career Teaching (2024)
The A–Z of Student Wellbeing (2025)
The A–Z of Addressing Disadvantage (2025)
The A–Z of Primary English (2025)
The A–Z of Good Governance (forthcoming)
The A–Z of Primary Leadership (forthcoming)
The A–Z of Independent School Leadership (forthcoming)